Through Stress and Strain

"What is this, my son?"

Emma Leslie
Junior Church History Series

Through Stress and Strain

A Story of the Huguenot Persecution

BY
EMMA LESLIE

Illustrated by
C. A. FERRIER & J. F. W.

Salem Ridge Press
Emmaus, Pennsylvania

Originally Published
1887
The Religious Tract Society

Republished 2009
Salem Ridge Press LLC
4263 Salem Drive
Emmaus, Pennsylvania 18049

www.salemridgepress.com

Hardcover ISBN: 978-1-934671-34-4
Softcover ISBN: 978-1-934671-35-1

PUBLISHER'S NOTE

In *Through Stress and Strain* Emma Leslie uses a difficult time in the history of the French Church to remind us of the importance of grounding even young children in the truth of God's Word. Whether or not families today are faced with a government physically taking their children away, the world with its allure is always trying to steal the hearts of Christian children. Only as our children know God's Word will they be able to stand firm in the faith.

Ultimately we are reminded that the faith of the next generation cannot be taken for granted, but as parents truly train up their children in the way that they should go, we can be confident that they will not depart from it.[1]

Daniel Mills

December, 2009

---

[1] Proverbs 22:6

HISTORICAL NOTES

King Louis XIV: Born in 1638 A.D., Louis became king of France at the age of four. His main goal as king was to increase his own power and he built himself a magnificent palace in Versailles. Louis ruled France for seventy-two years until his death in 1715.

Huguenots: The French Protestant Christians during the sixteenth, seventeenth and eighteenth centuries were known as Huguenots. They were followers of the teachings of John Calvin and had many conflicts with the Roman Catholic Church.

Edict of Nantes: In 1598, King Henry the IV of France issued the Edict of Nantes. This edict, or decree, allowed the Huguenots one hundred cities in which they could have religious freedom. In 1685, King Louis XIV revoked the Edict of Nantes, and in the persecution that followed, 200,000 Huguenots fled from France.

France in the 17th Century

CONTENTS

Chapter		Page
I	The Village Home	1
II	A Cruel Law	18
III	The Stranger's Visit	34
IV	Converting the Huguenots	52
V	At the Convent	71
VI	A Dangerous Treasure	87
VII	At Nîmes	105
VIII	The Escape	124

ILLUSTRATIONS

"What is this, my son?"   *Frontispiece*

"He must attend mass!"   61

François caught his foot in a stone!   135

Through Stress and Strain

Through Stress and Strain

Chapter 1

The Village Home

IT was a lovely afternoon in the spring of 1666 that a weary-looking horseman alighted at a small roadside inn, and after calling for a stoup of wine for himself and some water for his horse, inquired the nearest road to St. Etienne, a small village on the lower plateau of the Cevennes.

All through the sweet, soft country of Languedoc the traveler had been brisk enough, noting the condition of the vines and of the promise they gave of a future

STOUP: *cup*
PLATEAU: *a high, flat area of land*
CEVENNES: *a mountain range in southern France*

harvest; but now he was looking weary. Although the landlord of the inn pointed out the best road for him to take, he seemed in no hurry to mount his horse again when he had finished his wine; and so, for lack of other customers to serve, the landlord thought he might glean a little news from this one.

"From Nîmes, messire? What news from Paris?" asked the host of the inn.

The traveler shrugged his shoulders and shook his head. "Louis the Great is Louis the Great still," he said in a mocking tone; but he looked curiously at the landlord as he spoke, to see whether his words conveyed more than their outward seeming, and then he said, "What news has reached this out-of-the-way corner of France?"

"Not much, messire. We have but few travelers during the winter; 'tis scarce worth opening the door, in fact; for, as you doubtless know, Huguenots are but poor

MESSIRE: *"my lord" in French; a title of respect*
HUGUENOTS: *French Christians*

The Village Home

customers to a wine-seller."

"And the village is Huguenot?" said the traveler, as if asking for information.

"Ah! peste is it. A poor-spirited lot, these people of the religion, with no feasts but Sunday, and that spent in hearing sermons and singing hymns, instead of a merry dance on the green, with plenty of wine to keep their feet going. If it was not for a few who are of the king's religion, and for some jolly father of the Church who comes this way to help them keep the saints' days, I might as well turn Huguenot myself. Ah! our king is not so devoted to the Church as he should be, or he would drive this monster of heresy from our land, now that he has all power in his own hands."

"Why, what more would you have?" exclaimed the traveler, in surprise. "The king has done more to harass these people than the late cardinal, and surely he was a faithful servant of the Church!"

PESTE: *like a plague*
HERESY: *views that go against accepted beliefs*
CARDINAL: *an important official in the Roman Church*

4   Through Stress and Strain

"Mazarin!"[1] said the innkeeper, with a contemptuous shrug and discontented grunt. "If Richelieu had but lived a little longer, he would have driven them out of France entirely. He broke their power when he took that stronghold of heresy, La Rochelle, and—"

"Nay, nay; Richelieu was too wise a statesman to try and impoverish France by driving away her most industrious workmen. I am a merchant, with an eye to the best goods. I can buy and sell, no matter whether they are produced by those of the religion or their Catholic neighbors; but I tell you, gossip, I have to look sharp when I am buying of a Catholic, or I may make a bad bargain, and be left with the worst article in the market on my hands."

The innkeeper laughed. "I am of the same opinion, and I've learned by experience too; and whenever I buy a bit of cloth in the village here, I always take care it comes from

---

[1] Cardinal Mazarin became chief minister of France in 1642, following the death of his mentor, Cardinal Richelieu.

The Village Home

a Huguenot loom, much as I hate the religion."

"It's the same with their wines and their silks, their glass and leather. I am always open to a bargain that I can sell again at a good profit, and I say it will be a bad day for France when we merchants can't get the top prices in every market, and we should be driven out of all if it wasn't for the Huguenots. Whether it is because they have about fifty more working days than their neighbors, I can't say; but I do know they put more heart into their work than most people," said the stranger, taking up his broad-brimmed beaver hat and replacing it on his head.

"And you have an eye for a good thing in cloth, and have come to see the winter's work of our villagers. You are only just in time, for our people will soon be moving with their flocks to the higher slopes of the hills; but perhaps it is silk you have in your eye.

GOSSIP: *friend*

6 Through Stress and Strain

Never was a better year for silkworms than this last has been, and, as usual, the Huguenots seem to have had all the luck, for they have reared twice as many as their neighbors," said the talkative innkeeper.

But whether it was cloth, silk, or silkworms that the merchant was in search of, or whatever his business might be, he did not seem disposed to talk about it; and finding that he could learn very little from the host of the inn as to what had actually been going on here lately, he soon mounted his horse again, and resumed his journey.

A pleasant, peaceful scene the village presented when the traveler drew near in the dusk of the evening. Each cottage stood in a garden or in a little orchard of mulberry trees. From some of the open doorways came the sound of the flying shuttle and the click-clack of the loom, as the busy workman finished his day's task by the waning light. Others were digging their gardens or

WANING: *dimming*

The Village Home

loosening the soil round the mulberry trees; while among the women and children were signs of packing up for the summer flitting to the higher pastures.

A lad about ten years of age, on his way from the little village shop, caught sight of the traveler as he passed, and instantly recognized him.

"Oh, Uncle, you have come at last! Mother was afraid you would be too late, for we go to the hills the day after tomorrow. But—but where is Jacques?" he asked, looking round as he spoke, as if in search of someone else.

"Jacques has not come," said the traveler shortly.

The boy did not wait to hear more; he felt too much disappointed to ask the reason, but ran on to tell the disquieting news at home.

"Jacques not come!" said his mother, who met him in the garden, and she went on to

FLITTING: *move*

the gate to meet the horseman, who was slowly coming up the road. He was looking cross as well as weary, and the woman grew alarmed as she caught sight of his face.

"Oh, brother! what is it? What has happened to our boy?" she said, anxiously laying her hand on the bridle as she spoke.

The man dismounted at once, and grasped her hand. "I began to fear I should be too late," he said.

"Yes, we expected you a week ago. But what of Jacques—where is he? Why is he not with you? It was a promise, you know, that he should come back for this summer on the hills."

"Yes, yes; but we cannot always keep our promises," said the man evasively, in a tone of vexation.

The mother's keen eyes saw there was something amiss, something to be kept from her as long as possible; and clasping her hands, and facing round upon the

EVASIVELY: *avoiding answering directly*
VEXATION: *frustration*

traveler, she said with whitening lips, "Is my boy dead? Has our father—"

"No, no; Jacques is as well as you are," said the man impatiently. "Let us go indoors, and I will soon explain why he has not come."

But he seemed in no hurry to explain the mystery. The horse was put up, greetings were exchanged, and the table set out for supper, but no word was said about Jacques, until one of the younger children, sidling up to her mother, whispered aloud:

"When is Uncle going to tell us about Jacques?"

"All in good time, Ninon. We will have supper first. Jacques is well; and that must content you for the present, little ones," said the visitor, feeling a little more at ease now; and he launched out into details of business and the political action taken by the Huguenots of Nîmes.

Intrigue and double-dealing was the occupation or amusement of everybody in France

---

SIDLING: *moving sideways*
INTRIGUE AND DOUBLE-DEALING: *treachery*

just now. It was in the air like an infection, and the astute Nîmes merchant had caught the contagion like the rest of his countrymen, and was ready to hope for all sorts of things from this nobleman being disgraced, and that one exalted in the favor of the king, although he knew that the power of the nobles was as much a thing of the past as that of the Huguenots themselves. But the stories he had to tell of this and that piece of wire-pulling seemed to fall flat in this simple household, and it was a relief to his brother when, the frugal meal being over, he could say, "Now let us go outside, and you can tell me how it is Jacques has not come with you," for he could see it was no good news his brother had to tell about the boy.

Once outside, the merchant's face changed, and he looked grave and anxious, as, laying his hand on the weaver's shoulder, he said, "I hope you will not blame me in this miserable business, Claude."

WIRE-PULLING: *puppetry; in this case efforts to control the government*

The Village Home

"You promised to take care of the lad, and I trusted you as one Huguenot with another," said the other shortly.

"Yes, yes, and I did take care of him all I could. He was a good lad, too—steady and industrious. It is the law, not the lad, who is to blame, Claude, and you must not be hard upon him."

"Why should I be hard upon him?" said the father, but he spoke in an unsteady voice, for he knew he had not heard all yet.

"No, it is not fair to be hard upon our children when so many temptations are offered them to take up the king's religion instead of our own," went on the merchant.

"What! what is that you say? my Jacques turned Catholic? I don't believe it! I'll never believe it!" exclaimed the father in an agonized voice, and staggering against a tree as he spoke.

"I don't believe he has really chosen the Catholic faith in preference to that in which he was brought up, but he has been incautious enough to say something, enough for our enemies to make a handle of—it does not need much to do that, you know—at all events, he has been taken away from me, and placed in a Catholic seminary, and the payment for his board and education there has been demanded of me."

"But—but Jacques is only thirteen; he cannot abjure his faith until fourteen, even by law," said the agitated father.

But the merchant shook his head. "The age has been lowered to seven, and Ninon there would be counted a Catholic tomorrow if she said, in the hearing of anybody that could report it to a priest, that she wished to know what the king's religion was. Some such incautious speech Jacques must have uttered, and—"

"But what does he say himself?" interrupted the father.

"Ah! that we shall never know, for I have not been allowed to see him. I missed him

ABJURE: *renounce*

The Village Home

from the counting-house one morning, and an hour or two afterwards was informed by a plausible old monk that my nephew had turned Catholic, and was sent to the school belonging to the Franciscan monastery, and that five hundred francs must be paid at once for his first year's stay there."

"But he must not stay there," said the father distractedly; "I would rather he should tend sheep, or work at the loom, and never go beyond our mountains all his life. He must come home again and content himself here."

"Claude, be reasonable. You know that if once it happens that one of our children falls into the hands of our enemies as Jacques has done, they never can return. It is cruel, unjust, say what you will, and I have been trying for years to get this law altered, but—" And here the merchant shrugged his shoulders, sighed, and applied himself to his snuff-box for consolation; while his brother, in his long white camise, just as he had left

PLAUSIBLE: *someone who seems believable*
CAMISE: *loose-fitting shirt*

the loom, stood leaning against the tree in an attitude of utter despair.

"If he had only died!" he gasped at length, "but to forsake his God and Savior and turn to this monkish mummery will break his mother's heart."

"Oh, you mustn't look at it in that way," said the merchant briskly; "such things are too common now to be thought much of. Besides—" But the words he was about to utter died on his lips as he looked at his brother's white face. Worldly counsel would be utterly lost upon Claude, he knew, and it would afford him no comfort to be told that his son might yet be a prosperous merchant, though he had forsaken his father's faith.

There were two distinct types of Huguenots now: the old-fashioned sort, like Claude, who clung to the simple truth as taught by Calvin, and those whom the exigencies of the times had made more accommodating in many things as regarded their faith; but they still gloried in the name of Huguenot,

THIS MONKISH MUMMERY: *these empty ceremonies*
EXIGENCIES: *urgent needs*

The Village Home

as affording them some shadow of political liberty.

In the time of Henry of Navarre, when that grand law of toleration, the Edict of Nantes, was granted to the Huguenots, they formed themselves into something like a political federation, and this had been still further developed since, so that now in the towns the Huguenots had constituted themselves into a distinct civil community.

There doubtless was good reason for this at the time, but it had a most disastrous effect upon the spiritual life of the Church, and in many places it degenerated into a mere political council, and its members were content to be Huguenots by profession and politics, caring little for the spiritual freedom so dear to their fathers.

Our merchant of Nîmes, Jules Marot, was a Huguenot of the latter pattern. His brother had noticed the change gradually creeping over him since he had left the old home in the Cevennes; and when he proposed to take his nephew and help him on in the world, the father had shrunk from the proposal at first. The boy himself was eager to go; the family was a large one, and the little village could offer no opening for him but weaving, silkworm rearing, sheep and cattle tending, or chestnut growing, each of which or two or three combined would only afford a frugal living with a simple, primitive mode of life, and in none of them did Jacques care to engage.

He longed for a more stirring life, where books could be met with, and the education which had been suddenly arrested a year or two before, by the banishment of the schoolmaster, carried on a little further; and so at last, after many prayers, it was arranged that Jacques should go to Nîmes for the winter, but return to his home in the spring to spend a few months on the hills with the sheep. By this arrangement the influence of his home would not be broken off all at once, thought

MODE: *way*
ARRESTED: *stopped*

the careful father, and his brother had willingly consented to the plan; but Jacques had gone to Nîmes only to be entrapped into a Catholic seminary, as so many Huguenot children had been before him.

Chapter II

A Cruel Law

JULES MAROT left his brother leaning against the tree, and walked on through the village, for he knew Claude would rather be alone for a little while; and the weaver, after watching him walk in the direction of the chestnut grove, turned towards the pile of ruins that lay in a field a little to the back. It was all that remained of a church and school that had stood here, until a year or two previously, since the reign of Henry of Navarre. The buildings had been pulled down, like many others in the land, because the title deeds could not be found when the King's Commissioner came to examine

A Cruel Law 19

them. It had been a bitter trouble and disappointment to the Huguenots thus to be deprived of their church and school, but the power of the king was absolute, and all pleading was in vain; so the schoolmaster was banished, and the pastor could only pay occasional visits to his flock. Claude Marot, thinking of all this, as he crept in among the ruins of the beloved sanctuary, burst into an irrepressible cry of anguish. Here lay the root of the present trouble; for if the school had been carried on, his Jacques would have been content to stay at home among his native hills; and at the thought of what had happened, the father's grief broke out afresh, and he threw himself on his knees and tried to pour out his heart in prayer to God. But even prayer failed to comfort him under such a calamity as this. If his boy had been idle, or had fallen into any other kind of trouble, he might have found strength and consolation where he had so often found it before; but he could discover no ray of light in this darkness, and so it was with a heart bowed down by sorrow and despair that he went home to tell his wife the sad news.

The children were in bed, and Madame Marot was busily sewing by the light of a resin candle when her husband got back. She met him as he lifted the latch of the door, for she knew by the sound of his slow, heavy footsteps as he came up the garden path that some new calamity had befallen them. Alas! scarce friend or stranger came to their hills now without bringing news of some fresh trouble for the Huguenot inhabitants, either public or private. Every month or two there was some new enactment to harass and disturb these peace-loving people, and to make the difference between them and their Catholic neighbors more marked. Since their church and school had been destroyed, they had been forbidden to

RESIN: *pine sap*
MARKED: *obvious*

sing hymns with their cottage doors open; and as this was almost a necessity for the sake of light and ventilation at that time, the grievance was no small one.

But the pressure of these general and public troubles was as nothing to the Marots compared with what had now befallen them in the loss of their son, and all else was forgotten now. In a few bitter words the father told what his merchant brother's news had been, and for a time his wife too was overwhelmed with grief; but she was the first to rally when she saw her husband's despair. "We must carry this trouble to God with the rest," she said through her tears.

"Ah! but there is no hope for us in this," Claude replied, with a groan.

"No hope!" exclaimed his wife; "is not our boy still in God's hands, though the priests of Baal have him in their power? Nay, nay, my Claude, that is not like you. Our Jacques needs our prayers more than ever he did before. Let us pray that if his faith has failed in this time of temptation, he may yet be restored to us, and to the faith he has learned of us."

"Restored!" exclaimed her husband impatiently; "if he came back tomorrow he would be condemned as a relapsed heretic, and be banished from France forever."

Madame Marot sighed, but went quietly to a little outbuilding where she could pour out her soul in prayer to her Heavenly Father for her son, and husband too, for his trust in God seemed failing under the stress of this great trial. When she went back she found the merchant had returned, and the two brothers were deep in talk as to what could be done to rescue Jacques from the hands of the priests.

"I don't blame you, Claude; I'm glad to see you pluck up a little spirit. Come back with me to Nîmes, and we'll try what can be done by our town councilors. The king

RELAPSED HERETIC: *someone who has gone back to believing heresy*

must be made to know he has got some subjects who will not bow to all his whims," said the merchant, as Madame returned to the sitting-room.

She looked at her husband and then at her brother. "Is it not your town councils and—and this trying to have a government of your own, that provokes the king to make all these cruel laws against us?" she ventured to say.

But the merchant disdained to argue such a point. "You leave that to us," he said coldly. "Claude has decided to go back with me to Nîmes tomorrow, and to claim Jacques, in spite of this last new law. Surely you can have nothing to say against that, Babette?"

"I will speak to neighbor Pechel first, and ask him to see you safely to the hills before I go," said her husband.

"I shall go safely enough with the neighbors; it is not for that I fear," said Madame Marot, but her voice trembled as she spoke.

"What is it, then?" said her brother-in-law a little impatiently.

"It is your town councils that you talk so much about. I don't know how it is, but Huguenots of the towns have grown to be somehow different; instead of trusting in God and looking up to Him in time of trouble, you depend upon what your councils or assemblies can do for you," said Madame Marot.

It was true enough, although the merchant seemed greatly offended at being told the unpleasant truth. The fervent piety that had once distinguished the Huguenots was fast disappearing, and rivalries, jealousies, and worldly ambitions were taking its place in too many hearts. This had brought about a want of union for common self-defense; and their power had been still further weakened by continual strife, which was diligently fomented by the agents of the Government.

Madame Marot may not have understood

PIETY: *devotion to God*
WANT: *lack*
FOMENTED: *promoted*

the political aspect of affairs, but she knew that the spirit that had animated their ancestors was fast disappearing, and she felt that they were cutting themselves off from the source of all true strength and help, in seeking it from man instead of from God.

"Claude, let Jules try, an he will, to get our boy back; but won't you seek the help of God alone in this trouble?" she said, with a gasping sob.

The merchant looked astonished.

"You are the boy's mother, and yet refuse to lift a finger to save him!"

"No, no," she gasped, "it is not lifting a finger, but giving up my husband too. I am afraid of your city, Jules; it kills prayer, and hope, and trust in God. Besides, Claude can do no more than you. Would your council give more heed to a man in a camise than to you in a black cloth doublet and beaver hat? It is not likely," added Madame Marot.

The weaver and merchant looked at each

AN HE WILL: *if he is willing*
DOUBLET: *tight-fitting jacket*
BEAVER HAT: *a hat made of beaver fur*

other in surprise, for neither had expected to meet with such opposition as this; but the hint about Claude going to Nîmes with him in a weaver's camise, or smock frock, was enough for the merchant, and he soon began to suggest a compromise.

"Perhaps Babette is right, after all," he said, turning to his brother. "I will go on to Nîmes tomorrow, and lay the matter before our council, and you can follow, Claude, after you have taken Babette and the sheep safely to the hills."

"Yes, yes; spend a few days with us in the hills," said his wife eagerly, as she lifted down the clumsy-looking New Testament from its shelf, and laid it open before her husband.

She had found the parable of the lost sheep, and with his mind full of the loss of his own son, Marot began to read, almost unconscious of what he read at first; but the tender pathos of the father's welcome to

SMOCK FROCK: *a loose outer garment*
PATHOS: *emotion*

his long-lost son brought to his mind a few words that had been spoken by their aged pastor only a few days before: "It is a picture of God's dealings with us, His erring, willful children, and He is as ready to welcome us back as the father of the parable," said the old patriarch, as he leaned upon his stick and spoke a few words to those who gathered round him, as he went to pay his weekly visit to the ruins of their little church.

There could be no regular service, or sermon even, among the scattered stones and timber, but somehow it had come to be the custom for a few to follow the old man when they saw him wending his way towards the spot hallowed by so many sacred memories. Only a few at a time dared to go, and so the village divided itself into companies, and took it in turns to group themselves round the patriarch pastor, who had come to end his honored, useful life among his native hills.

PATRIARCH: *honored leader of the church*
WENDING: *making*
HALLOWED: *made holy*

The whole Huguenot community held him in no common reverence, and the words he had so lately spoken came to Claude Marot's mind now, bringing comfort and strength, and after kneeling in prayer, he said, "I will go and talk to Pastor Dupuy about it tomorrow. He will see some light in the darkness, if any man can."

Alas! when he went to the little rose-covered cottage the next morning, he heard, to his dismay, that the faithful servant of God had entered into his rest. Without any warning, any premonitory illness, the aged saint had passed away in his sleep.

"Jules, you loved the old man, you will stay for his funeral. None of us will go to the hills until this is over now," said Marot, when he had told the news.

The merchant shook his head, but he was not unmoved. "I would gladly stay, but why should I take the place of a better man? It

NO COMMON REVERENCE: *great reverence*
PREMONITORY ILLNESS: *illness warning beforehand of his death*

A Cruel Law

will be hard enough to choose the twelve who may follow him to his grave, without me staying to oust one who has a better right to do it than I have."

"What do you mean?" asked Madame Marot through her tears. "We shall all follow dear old Pastor Dupuy to his grave."

But the merchant shook his head again, as he said bitterly, "But the law—you forget the law, Babette."

"What law? Who would wish to prevent us from mourning our Maître Dupuy?" she asked.

"Have you not heard of that, either—that no more than twelve persons may attend a Huguenot funeral or wedding?" exclaimed the merchant in surprise.

Husband and wife both shook their heads. "It cannot be true!" exclaimed the weaver at length. "What harm could we do going to a funeral? If it were not for the power of Colbert the Chancellor, we should not have

OUST: *force out*
MAÎTRE: *"Master" in French*

even the liberty to live," he added with a cynical bitterness.

The talking of these galling restrictions seemed to change the merchant again. He had begun to grow gentle and kindly among the children of his brother's family, but now his face again assumed the hard, defiant look that had so repelled little Ninon and the rest of the children when he first came.

"I can't stay to talk about it, Claude," he said fiercely. "I remember Maître Dupuy, and how he talked to us, when we were lads, of the Huguenot soldiers whom he led into battle under Henry of Navarre, to the sound of our ancestors' hymns. I would gladly stay to his funeral, as a Marot and a Huguenot should; but see, it would but excite suspicion and enmity against you all, so I will mount my horse and return to Nîmes at once, and do you follow as soon as you have settled Babette and the children on the hills."

CYNICAL: *scornful*
GALLING: *irritating*
ENMITY: *hostility*

A Cruel Law

"We shall not go until after the funeral," said Madame Marot, "so Claude cannot reach Nîmes just yet."

"I will do all I can in readiness for his coming, but I have not much hope, Babette."

"Nor I, in your council," she replied. "God only can help our boy, and prayer will do more than any council can; but Claude shall come to Nîmes, never fear."

This was said while the horse was being saddled, and in a few minutes Jules was riding out of the village again.

It was well that he went as he did, for an hour after he had departed a message was brought to Claude, couched in most uncourteous language, and which would not have failed to rouse the angry resentment of the Nîmes merchant. It fully confirmed his statement concerning the law and Huguenot funerals, for Claude was informed that only twelve would be allowed to go to the cemetery when Dupuy was laid in the

COUCHED: *worded*

grave, and all beyond this number attempting to follow would be arrested, either men, women, or children.

"We will obey," said Claude to the messenger; for although the Huguenots were in a majority at St. Etienne, they were so closely overlooked by those placed in authority over them that they dare not venture to set the laws at defiance.

It was very hard, though. There was not a family in the village but loved and reverenced the saintly old man, and longed to pay the last tribute of respect to his memory by seeing him laid in his resting-place. His successor, too, their present pastor, would have a word to say to them at the grave, and his visits now were all too infrequent to make this opportunity one lightly to be lost. After some consultation, it was arranged that none of the families should remove from the village to the higher pastures until after the funeral, and that a petition should

OVERLOOKED: *watched*
SET THE LAWS AT DEFIANCE: *break the laws*

A Cruel Law

be presented, asking for a relaxation of the law in this instance, that all who wished might be present in the little cemetery, when Pastor Dupuy was laid in his grave.

The petition was duly drawn up, and presented with all becoming formality, but not the slightest relaxation of the rule imposed by law could be obtained. Twelve only might follow the body to the grave, and these in silence. There must be no singing of hymns, and only a few words were to be spoken at the open grave.

So the sorrowing friends had to content themselves with standing at their open doorways or garden gates, as the simple funeral, with its twelve mourners, passed by; but the harsh restriction was felt none the less keenly because it was borne in silence.

Chapter III

The Stranger's Visit

THE day following the funeral was a busy one at St. Etienne. At the first glimmer of dawn everybody was astir, and the children were in a state of blissful excitement over the business of starting for the upper pastures.

Mules had to be laden with the stores of food and sundry articles of furniture that were to be taken to the little châlets on the upper slopes; and now the bedding was tied up and added to the load, the baby's cradle placed so that it could be utilized on the journey, room made for the younger children to ride when they were tired, and for

SUNDRY: *various*
CHÂLETS: *huts*
UTILIZED: *used*

a few weakly lambs to be carried over the roughest part of the rugged mountain road.

Then the cattle had to be turned out of the byres, and the sheep gathered from the neighboring pastures, and a scrambling breakfast eaten in such a hurry that the watchful mother took care to have a basket packed with the scattered remains, which she knew would be called for before the first mile of the journey was over.

When at last all the packing was over, the cavalcade started; for this yearly exodus from the village was made simultaneously by those who were to spend the summer among the higher valleys and glens of the granite hills. Friends and neighbors liked to keep together as long as they could, for many of them would not meet again until autumn winds and threatening snow drove them back to the village once more.

The little summer châlets, nestled in the winding green valleys, were separated by

BYRES: *cattle sheds*
CAVALCADE: *procession*

the barren hills or overhanging cliffs, involving a roundabout journey of some miles; and although the travelers might often hear a neighbor's horn reverberating along the mountainside, it was not often they saw anyone but their own families, except the pastor, who paid them occasional visits, and brought them news of their friends scattered over the adjacent hills and glens.

But it was a busy, happy life, in spite of its monotony. Nobody had time to feel dull, for the children were either out in the fields looking after the cattle and sheep, or helping their mother in cheese and butter making at home, so that the day was scarcely long enough for all its tasks. When night came, and the family gathered together for the evening meal and to listen to the reading of God's Word, they were healthfully tired enough to enjoy sitting in a group at the châlet door, while they sang some of Clement Marot's hymns, and watched the

REVERBERATING: *echoing*
ADJACENT: *neighboring*
MONOTONY: *lack of variety*

stars appear one after the other in the deep azure sky.

It was a life leaving room for thought and mental growth; for while watching the sheep, or keeping the meek-eyed cattle from straying, there was nothing to hinder but much to help the mind to expand, alone with God and nature, free from distracting care, and under the stimulating teaching of their Huguenot pastors.

Doubtless this freedom and the healthful natural life lived by these people, contributed largely to that development of genius which in every department of life so distinguished them.

They were at liberty to think for themselves—not within the rigid lines laid down by the Romish Church, but with the glorious liberty of the children of God, as revealed in the Bible, which was their rule of life and faith. That this freedom of thought should branch out in all directions—mechanical,

CLEMENT MAROT'S HYMNS: *Clement Marot translated the book of Psalms into French in the 1500's.*

mental, and political—was but a natural outcome of the ever-springing fountain within; and but for the suicidal and repressing policy of Louis XIV, would, under the God-fearing guidance of the Huguenots, have found its natural development in the advancement of art, literature, and commerce, as well as of political independence, and would have lifted France to the highest pinnacle of greatness, while saving her from ages of anarchy and misery.

The liberty to sing their own hymns was dearly prized by the Marots. Here, in the loneliness of the upper valleys of the Cevennes, under the shadow of Mont Lozère, they could raise their voices without fear of offending any Catholic ears, and but for downright sleepiness they would have sat in the doorway and sung through half the night. But the careful mother would not allow this to continue too long.

"Now, François, go with Father to the

ANARCHY: *political chaos*

byre," she said, touching her boy on the shoulder as she spoke. "If he should go to Nîmes, you will have to see to the cattle by yourself."

There was a wistfulness in her voice as she spoke, and she looked at her husband pleadingly.

She hungered with all her soul for news of Jacques, but she dreaded this journey to Nîmes, and feared that little good would come of it.

But Marot was determined to go, and having seen his family fairly settled in their summer quarters, he set off one morning at daybreak on his long tramp to the city.

But before leaving he took François aside and bade him be careful how he answered any stranger he might see during his absence. "Keep the secret of our glens and valleys as you would your life, my boy, and say no word of the caves under the hills. Should you be asked the way to other châlets, point out the beaten mule-track, but not a word must be spoken of the hidden glens in the fastness of our mountains."

Marot scarcely knew why he spake thus to the boy, but his mind was full of vague misgivings, and who could tell but a storm of persecution might burst upon them at any moment, and spies be sent among them to discover the secret hiding places of their mountains?

For a day or two François thought much of his father's words, but no one came to disturb his solitary rambles as he followed the sheep up and down the slopes of the little valley; and in a week the warning had almost passed from his mind, when an incident occurred that ought to have put him at once on his guard.

A stranger appeared at the entrance of the valley one day, not to inquire the road to the next châlet, but to announce himself as a young pastor, who had just re-

FASTNESS: *stronghold*

The Stranger's Visit

turned from studying at Geneva. The very name of Geneva inspired confidence, and François saw what he had not noticed at first, that he wore the dress of their pastors, and at once offered to take him to the châlet, that his mother might entertain him suitably.

But the stranger declined this offer. He was tired, he said, and would sit down to rest for a little while, and François should finish singing the hymn he had interrupted.

So the two sat down together on a jutting spur of rock, while the sheep nibbled the short, fine grass that grew all round the little hollow, and the boy's clear voice rang out once again as he sang one of those hymns that had so often led his Huguenot forefathers to victory or to death.

The stranger bit his lips as he listened, but he did not speak until the hymn was concluded, and then from singing they fell to talking about all sorts of things and

DRESS: *clothing*

places—Geneva, Paris, the king and his love for his people, and his great desire to benefit them in all things. Very little was said about religion; and yet before he left the stranger had contrived to fill the boy's mind with doubts and dissatisfaction at being so exclusively kept to the Huguenot faith, and more than once he expressed a wish to know something of "the king's religion," which the stranger assured him differed very little from his own.

After an hour spent in such talk, the stranger asked the way to the châlet of the Pechels, as he was anxious to reach that before nightfall, he said. Again François begged him to go and see his mother first, and partake of some refreshment with them, but he pleaded that he could not spare the time today; he would come again in a few days and tell them something of his stay in Geneva.

The lad went home full of the news about meeting the young pastor, and soon began to look out for his return, leading the sheep so often to the same spot at the entrance of the valley that at last the place was almost bare of herbage, and, much to his disappointment, he was obliged to take them in another direction.

But during this time he had confided to his sister Ninon something of what the stranger had said, expressing his doubts as to the wisdom of his father and mother in not letting them know all about the king's religion.

"I don't know," said Ninon; "Father and Mother must know best what is good for us, and dear old Pastor Dupuy often said it was a soul-destroying religion. I wonder a young pastor from Geneva should set you wishing to go and see mass," she added.

"Oh, I only want to know what it is like," said François; "of course I am a Huguenot, and shall always be one; but still I do think we ought to know a little bit about the king's religion."

HERBAGE: *edible plants*
MASS: *the Roman Catholic church service*

Madame Marot heard something of her boy's dissatisfaction, but her mind was too full of anxious thought concerning her husband and his journey to think much about it for some time.

Marot was absent about a month, and then he returned looking weary and anxious, and ten years older than he did a few months before. His wife was struck with the change in him, but before asking any questions she hastened to prepare a substantial meal, for she knew he was tired out with his last walk over the rugged mountain road that was little better than a mule-track. He had stopped at the village to rest for a day, at the house of a neighbor, and heard that there was a whisper abroad about Jesuits being sent among the Huguenots of the surrounding districts.

"Have you seen any strangers in the neighborhood?" he asked, as he sat down to the table.

JESUITS: *Roman Catholic missionaries*

The Stranger's Visit

"No," replied his wife. "A young pastor from Geneva met François one day at the entrance of the valley, but he was too tired or too anxious to proceed on his journey to come here. Now tell me something of what you have been able to do for Jacques," she said.

The father shook his head. "Very little, very little," he said, "for when I got to Nîmes I found the whole place in a ferment over a proclamation that had just been received from the king, forbidding Huguenots from practicing either as lawyers or doctors. Of course Jules and his fellow-citizens were very angry, and there was much debate over the subject; but there is no true union among our brethren now, and union is our only strength. When everybody is looking out for himself, and cares not to sacrifice aught of ease or comfort or ambition for the common good, what hope is left for us?" and Marot heaved a deep sigh as he spoke.

FERMENT: *turmoil*

"And you heard nothing of poor Jacques?" said his wife, her eyes slowly filling with tears. What was it to her now to hear of the degradation of all who professed the Reformed doctrine, while her boy, her darling, had been snatched from them, to be brought up in what she regarded as the soul-destroying superstition of Romanism!

"I could learn no more than Jules had already ascertained—that he had been sent to some Franciscan school near Paris, and that the cost of his stay there must be paid somehow."

"Oh, Claude!" was all his wife could utter for some minutes. They were but peasants, and though by thrift and hard work they knew nothing of actual poverty, such a drain as this upon their very slender savings would make all the difference between carking care and working with heart made light by hope. They had an object to save for too, and that was to purchase a little farm

DEGRADATION: *putting down*
ASCERTAINED: *learned*
CARKING: *burdensome*

The Stranger's Visit

on the lower slopes of the Cevennes, so that when they grew too old to climb to the mountain fastnesses for the summer pasturage of their cattle, their own fields would afford them what they needed, while they still could live within sight of the granite hills so dear to their hearts. It was but a passing thought, however, that was given to this side of their trouble. To have had Jacques back they would gladly have endured any privation. It was the thought that their boy would be driven to bow the knee to the Baal of Romanism, perhaps even come to love it at last, that was so great a trouble.

The news of the father's return soon brought all the children in, and then he turned out a capacious pocket that had been stored with little presents sent from Nîmes by Uncle Jules. Even Madame Marot had been remembered, but she scarcely knew what to do with such unwonted finery as several yards of velvet ribbon, even though

PRIVATION: *lack of comforts and necessities*
CAPACIOUS: *spacious*
UNWONTED: *unusual*

it was of sober black. "What can I do with it?" she said, holding it out at arm's length.

"Well, everybody seems to wear it at Nîmes," said her husband, a little amused at his wife's perplexity. "Put it round Ninon's caps and your own," he added.

But Madame Marot shook her head. "What might be suitable for the wife of a citizen would not do for us," she said sensibly. "Clean linen caps are for peasants, and with these I shall always be content." So the ribbon velvet was put away carefully, though Ninon looked eager and wistful, after her father's suggestion that her caps should be trimmed with it.

With the father's return the flocks were led further into the recesses of the valley, and the hope François had indulged of seeing the strange young pastor grew fainter and fainter, as the weeks went on and he did not come. But he did not forget what had been said in that hour's interview. The

The Stranger's Visit

stranger had contrived to instill such doubts into the boy's mind, that often as he lay on a grassy slope watching the sheep, his mind was busy in turning over the statement of the young pastor that, in all essentials, there was no difference between the "king's religion," as it was called, and the Reformed Church; and François often wished that he could know what the king's religion was. If he had gone to his father with the doubts and difficulties that now beset him, much would have been made clear to his mind; for Marot, though only a farmer-weaver, was well-grounded in Huguenot theology, and could have made it clear to the boy that so far from being alike in essentials, the Reformed Church was to the "king's religion" as light to darkness, freedom to bondage.

During this summer the community only received one visit from their own accredited pastor, and he was surprised to hear that a young student from Geneva had been

ACCREDITED: *official*

visiting among his flock. He had heard of him at other places, and he was not without some misgiving as to his errand; but he forbore to awaken fresh anxiety in the mind of Marot, when he found him so overwhelmed with trouble concerning Jacques. He was not the only father he had to comfort and console under this cruel abduction of their children; for this plan was being pushed with such vigor by the Jesuit advisers of the king, that hundreds of Huguenot children were now being educated in Catholic schools, while their own were being gradually closed, or so curtailed in the list of subjects that might be taught as to be little better than elementary schools.

It was a gloomy outlook for the Reformed Church of the future, and the pastor had little news that was cheering to impart.

Open persecution, he said, would be less disastrous than the policy that of late had been adopted towards them, when with the

ABDUCTION: *kidnapping*
CURTAILED: *reduced*

The Stranger's Visit

defection of Turenne, Pellisson, and other great Huguenots before them, so many were induced to yield an outward conformity to the fashionable creed, when not only advancement in their professions, but the very exercise of those professions, were dependent upon their yielding.

It was all very hard to bear in quietness. And yet the numerous harassing laws issued against the Huguenots served rather to divide than to promote union among them, so that Marot almost wished for the days of old, when Coligny led their forefathers as one man to victory or death.

DEFECTION: *desertion*
CREED: *set of beliefs*

Chapter IV

Converting the Huguenots

THE return of the people from the hill pastures to their winter quarters in the village had always been something of a festival, for pleasant as it might be to go to the little lonely châlets in the midst of the green rifts of the hills, it was, after all, more joyous to meet neighbors and friends once more whom they had not seen all the summer; and as one party after another arrived, a merry shout of greeting went up from the children, and everybody ran to their garden gates to welcome the newcomers, whoever they might be.

The Marots and the Pechels were the first to get back this year. A sudden snow shower,

RIFTS: *openings*

Converting the Huguenots 53

that fortunately had not lasted long, drove the former home in hot haste, and they arrived after nightfall, when only the red smoky light from the resin candles, shining through two or three cottage windows, gave them welcome, instead of the usual joyous shouts of the children, "The Marots have come! There's Ninon, there's François, there's baby Antoine," as each in turn came in sight, and were hugged and kissed by welcoming friends, and carried into a neighbor's house while their own was got ready for them.

But this homecoming was so different, and Ninon, with tears in her eyes, exclaimed, "Nobody is glad to see us now."

"Foolish child! no one expects us, because the snow came so soon this year. François, run on and tell the Aubins we have come," said Madame Marot.

But although she spoke cheerfully, it was with an effort, for she could not but feel that this was a dreary homecoming, in spite of the warm welcome the Aubins gave them as soon as they recognized François at the door. The children were at once carried in to the light and warmth, and the *pot au feu* being ever on the stove, a bountiful meal was soon prepared for the travelers; while everybody who had heard the news came to give their help in unpacking and getting the cottage ready.

It was a busy hour, and not so pleasant working by the light of the flaring, smoking resin candles as by daylight; but it was over at last, and the sleepy, tired children put to bed, and there was time to exchange a word of news with the neighbors.

"Do you know what is being said here, Marot?" asked one, when he and Claude came in from the byre together. "Our neighbors of the king's religion are boasting that there won't be many Huguenots come home from the hills this year, for so many have been converted by the preaching and

POT AU FEU: *a pot of stew kept always cooking over the fire with new ingredients added as necessary for each new meal*

Converting the Huguenots

teaching of the Jesuit fathers who were sent amongst them, that our village church will scarce hold all who are expected at the first mass."

"I have seen no Jesuits," replied Marot; "they never troubled us, though I kept a sharp lookout for strangers after what I heard here."

"It may be but an idle boast," said his neighbor.

And then the subject ever uppermost in the mother and father's mind was once more discussed in all its bearings.

The next day the festival of the return commenced. The Pechels arrived in the afternoon, and an hour later another family; but, to the surprise of all, the few Catholic families belonging to the little community pressed forward to help and welcome the last comers.

This was not noticed at first, in the bustle of assisting the Pechels; for there had always

COMMENCED: *began*

been a friendly feeling between neighbors of the differing faiths; but when, after the unpacking, the Lestranges went to a Catholic neighbor's for their first meal, and the curé of the parish followed quickly after, every Huguenot in the village looked at each other in dumb amazement, not unmixed with apprehension.

Could it be that a family of St. Etienne had been bought over? Such things had been heard of, but it was always among people at a distance. Marot had heard from his brother that the king, acting under the advice of Pellisson, had ordered that as bishoprics fell vacant, they should not be filled up, but their revenues taken to form a fund for bribing such Huguenots as could be induced to do it to give up their faith, or at least to kiss a crucifix, and go to mass and confession, and thus profess themselves of the king's religion.

"A bribe of a hundred crowns would doubtless be a great temptation to some,"

CURÉ: *priest*
BISHOPRICS: *positions of bishop*

Converting the Huguenots

Marot said, with something like angry contempt; but his neighbors knew it was only too likely to be true. And so it proved, for not only the Lestranges, but two other families went publicly to mass the following Sunday, and professed themselves Catholics.

But the consternation about this was as nothing to that which followed during the next week. Scarce a Huguenot family but was served with a formal notice, demanding to know why one or other of them—mostly children, between the ages of seven and thirteen—had not attended mass the previous Sunday, they being Catholics.

In the case of the Marots, the demand was made on behalf of François, and the father's hair almost stood on end with fright and indignation when he heard it.

"François a Catholic!" he gasped. "No, no, Monsieur le Curé; why not say I am Catholic instead?" replied Marot when he could find his tongue.

CRUCIFIX: *statue of Jesus on the cross*
CONSTERNATION: *alarm and dismay*

Fortunately the curé of the parish, if ignorant and bigoted, was a kindly old man, who had always lived in peace with his Huguenot parishioners, and felt sorry for them now; and so he condescended to enter into something like an explanation with Marot. François had expressed a wish to know something about the king's religion to one of the holy fathers sent to convert the Huguenots, and so of course his name was enrolled, and he must attend mass, come to confession, and learn the use of his beads, like any other good Catholic, said the curé, taking a pinch of snuff and handing the box to Marot in token of amity.

But Marot shook his head. "There is some mistake," he said; "none of your Jesuit fathers came to our châlet last summer, though I hear they went to Lestrange's with some effect."

"Ay, ay; they went to every family in our hills, and a mighty gathering in to the true

BIGOTED: *intolerant of others' beliefs*
CONDESCENDED: *lowered himself*
AMITY: *friendship*

fold has followed," said the old man complacently.

"Begging your pardon, Monsieur; but I say I saw not one of these monks, nor my wife either," said Marot impatiently.

"But the lad—call the boy François named here, and let us learn if he met not with some stranger while he was abroad with the sheep," said the curé.

At the word "stranger," Madame Marot looked up from her task of wool-combing, and her heart almost stood still as she recalled what she had heard from François about the stranger from Geneva. "He met one of our own pastors one day," she said with a gasp.

The curé looked at her and nodded, smiling at her simplicity. "He was one of our holy fathers, instead of a Huguenot pastor, and that made all the difference," he said.

At the same moment François appeared, and his father called him in.

SIMPLICITY: *trusting nature*

"You had a young stranger come to see you while you were up in the hills," began the priest, while his father looked at him anxiously.

"Yes," answered the boy; "one of our own pastors from Geneva."

"And you told him you wished to learn the king's religion," said the priest, as he again applied himself to his snuffbox.

"I said I should like to know what the king's religion was," corrected François.

"Just so, and that makes you a Catholic."

"But I did not say it to you," uttered the boy in dismay; "I only spoke to one of our own pastors."

"One of our Jesuit fathers, who has undertaken to convert the Huguenots of this district," said the priest coolly.

The boy looked at his father for a moment, and then flew to his mother's side.

"Mother! Mother! I never meant it," he gasped, clutching at her gown, as if for protection.

"He must attend mass!"

Converting the Huguenots

Marot stood as one petrified for some minutes, and when he did speak it was easy to see that it was a hard struggle to subdue his anger.

"This is a cruel law to take children from parents, and by force compel them to be brought up in a faith they hate," he said.

"I did not make the law, my friend," said the priest, not unkindly; "but see that the boy comes to mass and confession," he added, and with a nod he left the cottage.

"I'll go and warn some of the others," said Marot, as the door closed. "It shall never be said that we sent our children to mass." And as the priest closed the garden gate, Marot went out at the back door.

"Mother! Mother! what shall we do?" exclaimed François, kneeling by his mother's side, and laying his head on her shoulder.

She laid her work away, and looked at her boy with a face of speechless agony. "You will be taken from us!" she gasped. "I feel it, I know it. Oh! my child, my François, that you should be made to renounce the religion of your ancestors—a Marot too!"

"I will not, I will not, Mother," said the boy. "I am a Huguenot, and—"

"Alas! alas! but you are already reckoned a Catholic," wailed his mother.

"But, Mother, you always told us God looked at the heart, and He sees I am no Catholic," said François earnestly.

The poor woman dried her tears, and looked into her boy's eyes. "You are right, François," she said. "Never, never forget that God looks through all outward shows of things, right into the heart, and we too must look through all—even our dear hymns, and the precious Word of God itself—up to the face of God. My boy, you will have to leave us soon and go to some Catholic school or convent, and learn what the king's religion is. Ah! my boy, you will find it is darkness; veil over veil, hiding the face of God our Father, and Jesus Christ our Savior; but remember

CONVENT: *monastery*

this, God can see through it, straight down into your heart; and if you cherish that thought, you will be able to look through it too, up into the face of God. Think of this always, my François. Never mind other things. Don't try to remember or to think whether anything that is taught you is Huguenot or the king's religion, but look through everything, up to God Himself. Remember what we have sometimes seen up among the hills. A thick, dark cloud has hung over all the lower valleys, completely hiding the sun; but when you have got to the higher slopes, the cloud was below you, and the sun was shining in all its glory. Never forget this picture that you have so often seen, and believe that God's face of love is ever shining upon you, and that all mediators, saints, Virgin, masses, everything that comes between God and your own soul, are but clouds to distort and hide the ever-loving face of God in Jesus Christ our Lord. It may be we shall not be able to talk of this again, François; none can tell how soon you may be snatched away from us; but remember, Mother and Father will ever be praying for you at home, and you must pray for yourself, and that God will comfort us in your absence. You will think of this, my boy," she added. "I never had the chance to say a word to poor Jacques before he was snatched away, but—"

"Mother! Mother!" interrupted François eagerly, "perhaps I shall see Jacques, if they send me to a convent school."

Madame Marot clasped her hands, and something like a gleam of hope shone in her anxious eyes. "Perhaps you may, my boy," she said. "God grant you may! for then it might be you could help each other to remember what we have been talking about. You would tell him all I have said, François. You must be careful to think of it all for his sake," she added with true insight, knowing that if this talk was to be treasured carefully in the

Converting the Huguenots 67

boy's mind, the having to do it for the sake of Jacques would be more likely to ensure its remembrance.

In a short time Marot returned, looking a little triumphant. Not a Huguenot father or mother in the whole community would send their children to mass at the bidding of the priest; and it was hoped that, as they would all make this bold stand, he would not push things to an extremity, as he was an easygoing man. Whether he would have insisted on this point or not, the villagers of St. Etienne never had the chance of knowing, for the next day the intendant of the district arrived, with authority to carry off all the newly professed Catholic children, and place them in convent schools, or send them on to Paris, to be similarly disposed of there.

Consternation filled every heart when this order was made known, but no one dared to resist it; and the parents had little time for

INTENDANT: *government supervisor*

more than a few hasty words of farewell, and agonizing prayers to God to take care of their darlings, ere the wagon that had been sent to fetch the children was drawn up on the village green. Amid tears and lamentations the little ones were driven away. The intendant himself on his gaily-caparisoned mule was in charge of the wagon, which was completely surrounded by a number of servants, so as to prevent all attempts at escape or rescue. It would be vain to try to describe the sorrow and mourning that filled the Huguenot homes of St. Etienne that night, for the cunning young Jesuit had entrapped so many of the children during that summer tour among the hills, that except in those cases where mother and father and all the children had professed themselves converted to the king's religion, scarce a family but was bereaved of sons and daughters—sometimes the only one had been taken, leaving the home desolate indeed.

GAILY-CAPARISONED: *brightly-decorated*
BEREAVED: *deprived*

Converting the Huguenots

It was the most bitter and most hopeless sorrow that could fall upon them—far more bitter than death would have been, for then they could have looked on with hope to meet their loved ones in the Father's home above; but to have them snatched away from their care and love, to be brought up in the belief and practice of error, instead of God's truth—this was far more bitter than death, and some could find little comfort even in prayer under this calamity.

It was so with Marot. Coming so soon after the loss of his eldest son, it seemed to crush him completely for a time; and it was with more of relief than dismay that his wife heard him declare that he should leave her and the children for a little while, go to Nîmes and get a peddler's pack well-stocked, and start in search of his boys. She looked amazed at first when she heard of the wild plan, but she did not oppose it, for any sort of action would be preferable to the present silent brooding over his sorrow; and although she could not bring herself to hope much from it, still comfort might come to him in this way at last. She could never hope for more now than to pray for her dear ones through the silent hours as she sat plying her distaff; but God had many methods of comforting His children, and if her poor Claude could find it in wearily tramping from town to town, she would not say him nay. For herself she would be safe enough with her work and her children among their old neighbors; and so the needful arrangements for her husband's departure were soon completed, and Marot set off to lay before his brethren at Nîmes the cruel wrong that had been inflicted upon him a second time.

PLYING: *working with*
SAY HIM NAY: *tell him not to*

Chapter V

At the Convent

"AND this is the king's religion? this is all I shall ever learn?" The words were spoken in a half-indignant, half-questioning tone, and the lad looked up at the young monk he was speaking to, as if he would compel him to answer.

"Is it not enough, my son?" said the monk. "But, hush!" he added the next minute, "the brethren must not hear you speak in this way of our holy Church;" and the two turned and walked along the cloisters together once more, and as they passed another group of monks he was talking volubly to the lad of *lauds* and *prime* and *vespers*.

CLOISTERS: *covered walkways surrounding a courtyard*
VOLUBLY: *continuously*
LAUDS, PRIME AND VESPERS: *official times of prayer*

"Yes, yes," interrupted the boy; "we go to all these services every day, and repeat hundreds of Latin words we do not understand; but what does it all mean?"

"That matters not to us, my son," said the monk meekly.

"But it does matter to me," said his companion impetuously. "I was brought here to study the king's religion, because I was told it was so much better than our own Reformed faith that the king had decided to put an end to most of our schools, and pull down many of our churches, as being wholly unnecessary, and only likely to divide our nation."

"Yes, that is it," said the monk. "Our king, Louis XIV, will be the greatest monarch France has ever had, by uniting both religions into one."

"Then why not teach us—let us see the difference in the two faiths?" exclaimed the boy.

IMPETUOUSLY: *suddenly, without thinking*

At the Convent

"Be not impatient, my son; it may be that—"

"Impatient! I have been here nearly a year, and was six months at Toulouse; but beyond learning to repeat a few prayers in Latin, chant a few psalms, and learn a little music, I know no more the meaning of the king's religion than I did before I came."

"Say not so, my son, for it would grieve many to hear you were other than a good Catholic now. Besides, why should you seek to know more? Be content with this, that they are both alike," concluded the young monk.

He had grown very fond of this young Huguenot lad, who had been committed to his care by the superior of the convent; and so long as the boy talked of his home in the Cevennes, and his work of tending the sheep during the summer, he was ready enough to listen, but too often lately the conversation had strayed to the subject of the king's

SUPERIOR: *head*

religion, and it was plain that the bright, eager youth, so anxious to learn all he could about everything that came in his way, was growing impatient and dissatisfied over the endless repetition of meaningless prayers that was dignified by the name of religion; and how to prevent this dissatisfaction from reaching the ears of the other monks often sorely taxed his ingenuity now.

It would only bring disgrace and punishment upon the lad for disobedience, if he was heard grumbling and questioning about everything that others were content to receive and believe as a matter of course; and so something like a tacit understanding had been arrived at between them, that these discussions should only take place when they were by themselves in the cloisters, or during recreation time, when the other brethren would be too much occupied with their own charges to pay much attention to them. A sore burden were these young

TAXED HIS INGENUITY: *tested his cleverness*
TACIT UNDERSTANDING: *unspoken agreement*

At the Convent

Huguenots to the monks, and what to do with them, how to repress their restless anxiety to be learning something or other, deprived the whole community of all peace and rest. Of course they could not be allowed to meet each other indiscriminately, without the watchful care of a monk to overhear all they might say, or they would simply uphold each other in their heresy, which it was the determined purpose of the king to eradicate from their minds. Officially they were all considered as Catholics now, and every child captured and sent to a convent school was tabulated as "converted," and so the monks must see to it that the conversion was completed.

They found this task very different from what they had anticipated.

These eager, all-alive Huguenot children had been so well-instructed, young as they were, by the pastors and schoolmasters, as well as by their own parents, that they would

INDISCRIMINATELY: *in an unrestrained way*
ERADICATE: *completely remove*
TABULATED: *recorded*

not be put off with platitudes about yielding obedience to the Church and those she had set over them, but wanted to know the meaning of this, and the reason for that, with a persistence that utterly bewildered the sleepy brains of the easygoing monks. If they had only ventured to exchange confidences with each other, these guardians of the young heretics would have found that their restless charges were all much alike. This, however, they were afraid to do, for fear of bringing upon themselves the anger of their superiors for permitting such questions to be asked, and so each tried to keep to himself as much as possible what he could not wholly restrain in his pupils.

The young monk who had been placed over Jacques Marot tried rather less repression than his brethren, because he had grown fond of the lad for his own sake, and also because some of the questionings had

PLATITUDES: *dull remarks*
REPRESSION: *restraint*

At the Convent

awakened an echo in his own heart, and he wondered whether there was an answer to be found for them anywhere. Jacques maintained that there was, and that a Huguenot pastor or schoolmaster could have solved the difficulty, and this seemed to make the boy grow more bitter every day.

"Why should our schools and churches be closed, if you have nothing to give us in place of them?" he asked during one of these discussions. He still grew angry sometimes, but not so often as at first, for he had ceased to blame his guardian individually, and began dimly to understand that the questions he asked were often troubling the young monk too.

"I was content to go to mass, learn my *Aves* and *Paternosters*, and leave all such questions, my son," he said in reply.

"But why should you?" said Jacques. "I am not, I cannot be; the Bible opens out such—"

"Ah! the Bible; but you see we never read

AVES: *"Hail" in Latin, the Catholic "Hail Mary" prayer*
PATERNOSTERS: *"Our Father" in Latin, the Lord's Prayer*

that, it is too difficult for the unlearned," interrupted the young monk.

"But it is the Word of God—His message to man about salvation through our Lord Jesus Christ, and therefore everybody should read it for themselves."

The young monk shook his head. "That book is the fruitful source of all heresy, my son," he said.

"What is heresy?" asked Jacques.

"Not believing what the Church teaches," promptly answered his guardian.

"But the Church—the Romish Church teaches nothing but to repeat a few prayers in a language we do not understand. What good can that do us?"

"We do not know; we have but to obey."

"That is what you always say, Father Eustace; but it does not satisfy me. I want to know—to understand things for myself. Our pastors say to us, 'Think about what we tell you; reason about it; read the Word of God,

At the Convent

and find out whether we speak the truth of God to you or not.'"

The young monk held up his hands in dismay. "You think, you reason, you question what a pastor or teacher may say?" he exclaimed in horror.

"Why not? God has given me my reason and mind to use, and why should I not use them by studying His Word, to find out what He would have me do, and whether other men speak the truth concerning Him?"

Such boldness completely awed gentle Father Eustace, and yet he could not help asking, "What does your Bible teach concerning prayers to the Virgin, do you know?"

"There isn't a word about prayers to the Virgin in it. I've read all the Gospels through to find out, for our schoolmaster told us one day that God had not commanded that adoration or worship should be paid to either the Virgin Mary or the saints, and I read the New Testament through to find out."

"But—but the Blessed Virgin is the mother of mercy, and the mother of our Lord," said the young monk, looking greatly shocked, although he condescended to argue with his pupil.

"She was a good woman, and God greatly honored her in making her the mother of His Son, but she is not the mother of mercy, except as she was His mother—the Lord of mercy, our blessed Savior, who died to redeem us from our sins because He loved us, and therefore had mercy upon us. That is where it seems to me your Church has made such a mistake: you have the Virgin and saints, and pay to have masses said for just what the Lord Jesus offers to us freely, if we will only accept it and give up our sins; salvation is His free gift."

Jacques had said more than he intended, but the words were spoken now and could not be recalled. He was afraid Father Eustace would be very angry—perhaps send him

At the Convent

for correction to one of the elder brethren, for the boys were often punished very severely for speaking of what they had learned from their own schoolmasters; but to his surprise the young monk only sighed, and then walked on in silence for some minutes. At length he said, "Such questions as these never disturb Catholic minds, and I did not know it was such things that occupied the Huguenots."

"What did you think about us?" asked Jacques, somewhat relieved.

"I thought of you as heretics, of course; but what the heresy was I cared little for, except that it was dividing France—you were trying to set up councils and parliaments of your own, and this could never be, you know."

Jacques had heard something of these councils while living with his uncle at Nîmes; but what he had learned at his mother's knee in the little village of the Cevennes was the distinctive form of Huguenotism that he understood, and it was this that he treasured and clung to, now that he was nominally a Roman Catholic.

It was something of a puzzle to the authorities what to do with and how to employ the eager lads, who were daily increasing on their hands. Of course they went to the daily services held in the chapel or church, but this did not occupy all the time; and as for the schools, these young Huguenots were so much ahead of average scholars of their age, and moreover had been so well-taught by their own schoolmasters, that the lessons given were mere play to them, and left them too much time to think of the heresy that they had been rescued from; and so at last it was arranged that some should be taught trades, and others engaged in studies that would fit them for professions.

It was decided that Jacques Marot should learn silk-weaving, and that looms and a

NOMINALLY: *in name*

At the Convent

master to instruct him and a few other lads should be set up at the convent, so that they could be under the supervision of the monks, and carefully guarded from any contact with the outside world.

When it first became known that these changes were in contemplation, Father Eustace was full of a nameless dread lest it should separate him from his charge, whom he had learned to love, and from whom he was learning so much, although as yet he scarcely recognized the change that was slowly taking place in his mind and heart.

But when he heard that he was to be with the party of weaver lads when they were at work, his mind was set at rest, for Jacques would be under his charge during recreation time still. He was always careful never to lead the conversation towards the lad's past life and what he had learned from his Huguenot teachers, but he did not try to repress it when Jacques seemed bent upon

IN CONTEMPLATION: *under consideration*

talking of it to him; and so by this means the germs of truth were sown in his heart, while no one—not even the young teacher or his guardian the monk—ever suspected what was really going on, silently and slowly, amid the monotonous routine of convent life, or the noisy clatter of the weaving-room. After a time, it was suggested that some of the younger monks should themselves learn silk-weaving, that they might instruct the boys without the aid of outside help, and so save the expense, and also the risk that must ever attend even this slight contact with the outside world.

It may be imagined that with all this care the anxious father would have small chance of seeing his boys, although he might travel all over France on his peddling expeditions; and the very fact that he and other poor Huguenots had adopted this mode of obtaining a livelihood, when it became known, made the authorities more watchful than

At the Convent

ever, lest they should gain access to their children.

But although Marot could never obtain a glimpse of his children, Jacques received news of his father in a roundabout manner. The weaver, who came from the adjacent village every day to teach the boys, one morning picked up the fragments of a worn old book. Like most good Catholics, he could not read, but the paper, he thought, would be handy to light a fire with, and so it was put into his pocket. Now, like all boys, the lads at the convent were fond of a practical joke; and when he was leaning over one of the looms, to give the young weaver some instruction, the draw-boy who had charge of the harness threads dexterously managed to pick his pocket of the book, and to pass it to Jacques Marot, who was standing near, sharing in the instruction, but who would not be called upon to take any active part in manipulating the loom just now.

DRAW-BOY: *boy operating the loom*
DEXTEROUSLY: *skillfully*

This gave him time to conceal the book in his doublet, without attracting any attention, for pockets were not allowed under convent regulations; and safe inside Jacques' doublet the book remained all day, for he and his companions forgot their joke soon after it was perpetrated. If the weaver missed his find of the morning he did not think it worth mentioning, for the old book was not of any value, at least to him, and so no inquiry was made about it, and everybody had forgotten the circumstance before night.

PERPETRATED: *committed*

Chapter VI

A Dangerous Treasure

WHEN Jacques Marot loosened his belt at bedtime Father Eustace who was standing near, saw a book fall to the ground. He picked it up, saying rather sternly, "What is this, my son?"

Jacques looked as much surprised as Father Eustace himself, until a half-suppressed titter from another boy close at hand reminded him of the morning's joke, for it was the draw-boy himself now laughing, who had handed the book to Jacques, and he at once confessed the trick he had played upon the weaver.

After a hasty glance at it, Father Eustace shut it up, and with a word of warning addressed to all the boys against playing practical jokes, he retired to his corner, where he usually sat reading his breviary, until his watch was relieved by another brother taking his place; for never a moment were these boys left alone, lest they should communicate with each other, and so keep alive their memory of the past.

Jacques' bed was nearest to the monk's corner, and as he lay awake looking at him, he noticed, that instead of his usual breviary, the young monk was eagerly reading the old book that had been filched from the weaver's pocket.

Listening intently, he soon became convinced that all the rest of the boys were fast asleep, and slipping out of bed he crept silently to the monk's side. So intent had he been, so deeply engrossed with what the pages of that old book had to reveal, that he did not hear the boy move until he was close at his side, whispering, "What is it, Father Eustace?"

BREVIARY: *the Roman Catholic book of prayers*
FILCHED: *stolen*

A Dangerous Treasure

He started and trembled for a moment, then turned the book towards him. It was the Gospel of St. John, and the margin was lettered and scored in a manner that Jacques instantly recognized.

"It is my father's!" he said with a gasp. "I have seen him put those marks there, as we sat watching the sheep in the upper valleys."

"You know what the book is?" said the young monk, allowing Jacques to take it in his own hand.

"Yes, yes; it is part of the New Testament. Oh! Father Eustace, let me keep it," he said imploringly.

But the monk could only shake his head. "My son, you know that you are not allowed to possess anything individually. All that is needful for you our superior provides, and anything beyond this can only be harmful to you."

"Harmful! but that is the Word of God—

LETTERED AND SCORED: *marked with notes*

the words of our Lord and Savior, whom you profess to worship."

"Hush! hush! my son. I do worship Him, and it is because you have made me long to know more about Him that I am reading this book, instead of taking it at once to Father Clement or the prior."

"But you will not take it to them! I can never see it or read it again if you do," pleaded the boy. "Say you will keep it for me, Father Eustace, and bring it here sometimes to read, so that I may see it. I may never see my mother and father again, and, oh! I should like to keep this book. See, over here is where my mother put some marks, when baby Claude died;" and Jacques turned to the verses commencing, "I am the resurrection and the life,"[1] and pointed out to the young monk his mother's marginal notes, thus convincing him that he spoke the truth in saying that the book had belonged to his parents.

[1] JOHN 11:25
PRIOR: *head of the monastery*
MARGINAL NOTES: *notes in the margins*

A Dangerous Treasure

Jacques saw that the young monk was troubled, and he went on, "Perhaps I shall never in all my life be able to get such a precious relic of the old life as this; you will let me keep it—you will keep it for me, Father Eustace, will you not?"

"You know not what you are asking, my son," said the monk, with a sigh. "This book is enough to consign us to the lowest dungeon of the convent if it was found in our possession," he said.

"But—but don't you want to read it, Father Eustace?" asked Jacques.

"I do indeed, my son, and I have thought I might perhaps keep it for a few days, but it must never go out of my possession; I must fasten it inside my frock, and sleep with it next to my hair shirt, lest at any time some of the brethren should search my cell in my absence."

"They would never dare to do anything so mean as that," said Jacques indignantly.

CONSIGN: *send*
HAIR SHIRT: *a shirt made of woven horse hair*

"You know nothing as yet of convent life, my son, and God grant you never may, for it is not what my dreams had pictured it," said his guardian; and then he told Jacques to go to bed, for the precious book would have to be put away at once, as the brother who was to keep the next watch would soon arrive; and Jacques saw, as he crept into bed, that his treasure was carefully concealed inside the folds of the coarse serge frock, but he was asleep before the older monk came to take the watch.

Every now and then a fresh batch of boys would arrive at the convent, while some would be drafted off to other places; but it soon came to be an understood thing that the boys who were learning weaving should continue as permanent pupils. There was great wisdom in this arrangement, considering the object in view; for the Huguenot children, if dissatisfied like Jacques with what these new schools could afford in the way of

SERGE: *a heavy fabric*

A Dangerous Treasure 93

positive teaching, were generally fascinated with the music and singing, the flowers and vestments, and splendid ritual of the Romish Church. The newcomers, fresh from country homes and the simple Huguenot service, would hear glowing accounts of the beauty of the chapel or church they would now attend, from those who were already here; for this sort of talk was not only approved but encouraged by the attendant monks, who were always within hearing, and reproved or commended, according as they heard their Church and its services described.

In this way the newcomers were weaned from old associations, and, in too many instances, from the faith of their ancestors, and at last grew to love what had at first been forced upon them.

It was, of course, a time of eager excitement in the community when a fresh draft of boys were expected, everyone being on the lookout for some friend or neighbor

VESTMENTS: *robes*

who might have been entrapped as they had been.

It may well be imagined what the feelings of Jacques Marot were when, among a company of new arrivals who were brought into the recreation ground one day, he recognized his own brother François.

The recognition was mutual, but both boys were too well-learned in the ways of their monkish guardians by this time to betray their secret, while they were being so narrowly watched as they knew they always were at these first meetings; for if it was discovered that brother, friend, or neighbor, was amongst the newcomers, the two were never allowed to meet after the first greeting, and in a few days one or the other was drafted off to another convent school. In this way all confidential communications were at once stopped, and the brothers, knowing this, were careful to avoid even looking at each other for the first few days, though each was

A Dangerous Treasure

longing to ask a hundred questions of the other.

It was bad training for boys, and such duplicity as the brothers now practiced would have been impossible to them while under their parents' charge; but the constant espionage to which they were subjected gave rise to a desire to outwit their guardians, and they often did it too, cunning as the monks were.

Now that there was so much to be gained by a little duplicity, who can wonder that the brothers resorted to it?—indeed, they carried it on so successfully, that although Father Eustace had the special oversight of them both, he never suspected that they were more than strangers to each other, until nearly a week had passed.

Then one day they both lingered behind in the weaving-room, after the teacher and other boys had left; and Father Eustace, turning round in the doorway to bid them

DUPLICITY: *deceit*
ESPIONAGE: *spying*

follow him at once, saw them clasped in each other's arms, François' head pillowed on his elder brother's shoulder, while he was sobbing out, "I've got a message for you from Mother; let me tell you soon, for it is hard to remember things in these places."

Father Eustace closed the door and came hastily forward, looking almost scared as he surveyed the two boys. "What is it? What is it?" he cried.

"Oh, Father Eustace! you will keep our secret," said Jacques imploringly; while François, thinking that all their care had been in vain, and that they would inevitably be parted now that their relationship had been discovered, dropped his head upon the edge of one of the looms, and gave himself up to despair and tears.

But Jacques had more hope in Father Eustace's well-known kindness, and besides, there was the secret of the hidden book which they shared between them. In answer to the young monk's groan of alarm, when he heard that they were indeed brothers, Jacques said quickly, "It will be but another secret between us, Father Eustace; and two secrets are as easy to keep as one."

The young monk sighed, but made no reply to this. "You must not stay here," he said quickly; "tell your brother to follow me at once, and you sit down and straighten those threads until I come and call you."

"Oh! thank you, thank you," murmured Jacques gratefully, for he knew their secret would be safe for the present, or he would not have given these directions, which were simply to prevent any suspicion being aroused in the minds of the other monks, which might be done if they were seen to leave the room together.

"You must consider yourself in disgrace for a little while," he whispered, as the younger Marot passed him; and his disturbed looks and the traces of tears still remaining on his face would fully bear out this suspicion.

But while Jacques was straightening out the harness of the loom, his heart was ascending in prayer to God that he and his brother might not be separated, now that they had once been brought together again. "Help us to help each other!" he prayed, "and to keep in mind our mother's message and what she so often taught us, to put our trust in Thee, our Father, and our Savior God."

It did help and comfort him to say thus, and for a time he could trust in God and Father Eustace that their secret would be kept; but still it was hard, very hard, to look at François as only a stranger, and never try to learn what that message was his mother had sent to him. He could pretty well guess what it was likely to be, but still he wanted to know the very words his mother had used, and how she was, and all about what had

A Dangerous Treasure

happened to bring François among them. But all these questions would have to wait, for it might be that months would elapse before anything like a confidential chat could be gained, though they slept under the same roof, ate at the same table, and worked but a few yards from each other.

For some time at least this semblance of their being strangers must be kept up, if only for the sake of Father Eustace, who had begged Jacques not to attempt to do more than whisper a word to his brother when they were at play, as he had reason to fear that he himself was under some suspicion by the authorities. If anything happened just now to confirm it, someone else among the brotherhood would be appointed as their guardian.

It was evident by the way in which this was said that Father Eustace would be very unwilling to give up the charge of the Marots now. "You have taught me so much," he

SEMBLANCE: *outward appearance*

murmured; "through you I have learned to love this precious Word of God; and yet, my son, it is a sore trouble to me," he added, laying his hand on the place where the book was concealed under his frock, "a sore trouble, for I know not how to reconcile this that I am doing with my vows of obedience."

It was not likely that Jacques could help him much in such a dilemma; he could only beg and urge him to keep the precious book safe, for monkish vows were nothing to him; but this fragment of God's Word was like a bit of his past life washed up to sustain him in the faith of his ancestors, and to give him hope for the future amid the troubled sea of his present surroundings.

He did not often have the chance of seeing it, except in Father Eustace's hand as he sat in his corner, for he often fell asleep, in spite of his determination to keep awake until the last. Sometimes, however, the sonorous breathing from every bed assured him

SONOROUS: *deep*

that the rest were fast asleep, and then he would slip out, creep to the monk's side, and holding the book between them they would silently read a chapter together.

Father Eustace foresaw that a time would come when it would be no longer safe to carry or to read the precious volume, and so he was preparing for it by committing chapter after chapter to memory. He had carefully read the whole Gospel through from beginning to end, for although torn and a good deal battered about, it was quite complete; and now, having once mastered it, he was picking out certain chapters and committing them to memory, and he advised Jacques to do the same, for fear the book should by some accident fall into the hands of the authorities. So whenever opportunity served, Jacques would creep out of bed and read over with deeper attention than ever the words that had been familiar to him all his life, but never so precious as they had become of late.

Weeks elapsed before he had the opportunity of hearing from his brother the message his mother had charged him to deliver; but one day, at the request of the weaver, Jacques was shut in the weaving-room to give his brother some instructions in the management of the harness threads, after the usual hours, and Father Eustace was directed to see that the two boys were not interfered with until their task was completed.

Fearful lest the boys should be surprised in the midst of their confidences by some over-officious brother, the young monk mounted guard outside the door, so as to be able to give them warning should anyone attempt to disturb them.

"Now, now for it; tell me, François, about that last talk you had with Mother, and the message she sent to me," said Jacques eagerly.

"Oh! Jacques, it has been so hard to remember it all this time. Why, it must be nearly two years since I left the Cevennes, and I

OVER-OFFICIOUS: *meddlesome*

A Dangerous Treasure 103

have never seen Mother or Father since."

"But what did she say? what did she say? We must not lose this precious chance now we have got it, for we may never have another. Now tell me what it was about," implored Jacques.

But François had to think a little before he could remember; at last, however, the well-known simile of the sun shining above the low-lying clouds, which they had both so often seen in the upper valleys, recurred to his memory, and he exclaimed, "I know it was this, that the love of God, like the sun, is always shining upon us."

Then, bit by bit, the whole scene came before him, and he told his brother that he need not think whether any doctrine was Huguenot or the king's religion, but to look right up through it to God Himself, for all books and teaching were but like clouds, some thicker and some thinner, but behind them all the love of God, like the sun at

SIMILE: *word picture*

noon, was ever shining, and that God, on His part, shone right through the clouds into men's hearts, and they must look up through all prayers and religious services to God Himself, and doing this faithfully and earnestly, they could not go far wrong.

"Ah! I must tell Father Eustace of that message; it is just what we need to remember here, François. Our mother is the wisest woman in the Cevennes, if not in all France," said Jacques admiringly; and then he turned to the harness threads again, to give the needed lesson, and ponder over his mother's words.

Chapter VII

At Nîmes

SEVERAL years have passed since Claude Marot first left St. Etienne, to start on his travels as a peddler, and to find some traces of his boys. With his pack he was fairly successful, both as a merchant and *colporteur* for the distribution of God's Word and Protestant books through the country districts that he visited; but of his boys he could hear no certain news. They were removed, as we know, from one convent to another; and the number of Huguenot children now being educated in Catholic schools made it difficult, almost impossible, to trace one particular child; but Marot tramped on from

COLPORTEUR: *a traveling seller of Bibles*

town to town and village to village, sometimes thinking he had discovered a clue to the whereabouts of his boys, only to find his hopes disappointed when he reached the spot.

There was one element of comfort amid all this disappointment, and that was the unanimous opinion of friends and foes alike, that the Huguenots who gave up their faith soon became heartily disgusted with "the king's religion" when they found out what it really was.

The Governor of Languedoc had mentioned it officially in these words: "It is certain that one of the things that holds the Huguenots to their religion is the amount of information which they receive from their instructors, and which it is not thought necessary to give in our schools. The Huguenots will be instructed, and it is a general complaint amongst the new converts not to find in our religion the same mental and

At Nîmes 107

moral discipline they find in their own."

Among these "new converts" Marot found ready customers for his books, to supply in some degree the loss of that "instruction" they dared not seek now, on pain of being arrested as relapsed heretics, but which their early training made them hunger for still.

But as the years went on, a change was wrought in Claude Marot that would have seemed impossible to one who had known him at St. Etienne. He was more fiercely Huguenot than ever, but all the sweet Christ-like graces of that faith had been forgotten. Injustice and disappointment, instead of driving him closer to God for help and consolation, had made him mistrustful, hard, and cynical.

He might not have become so unhappy had he remained at home with his wife and family; but out in the world, where he was continually hearing of some fresh aggression on their rights, granted under the Edict of Nantes by Henry IV, his anger was forever being aroused, and yet he could do nothing, for the Huguenots were so divided among themselves that no unity of action was possible between them, and they could only vent their dissatisfaction in impotent grumblings, or grow hard and cynical in their silence.

This was the way too many bore the troubles that were coming upon them, while others, like Madame Marot, betook themselves to God in prayer, and grew more gentle, more Christ-like, as they were pressed down by these earthly afflictions.

By her husband's desire she removed from St. Etienne to Nîmes, a few months after he took up the work of a peddler, and here she employed herself in making the elaborate cords, tassels, and balls of scarlet wool, that formed the fashionable mule trappings of that time.

IMPOTENT: *weak*

The little farm that had been the daydream of their lives for so many years was gradually being replaced in her mind by another hope, which would have been bitter as death to her but a few years before, but which alone could reunite her to her children now, and that was to leave France and make a home in the far-off England, where they would be free to worship God according to their own conscience.

It had become the refuge of many now, and Jules Marot had visited London in the way of business, and brought back a glowing account of the flourishing colony of Huguenots that had been established there, and at Canterbury and Norwich.

The reports that had been sent to them concerning Jacques and François first gave birth to this hope, for a demand was made for an additional payment, because they were learning the trade of silk-weaving, and this handicraft would be specially useful to them in England, and enable them speedily to make a home there. So while Ninon took care of the children, and made the *pot au feu* for dinner, Madame Marot spun and twisted, with quick, deft fingers, the scarlet wool that was to deck some wealthy citizen's mule gear; and often lifted up her heart in prayer to God for her absent boys, placed in such temptations that only God Himself could rescue them from.

But it was strange how utterly she trusted her children with God. Beyond the fact that they were living, and now learning a useful trade, she knew not aught about them.

Of course they must be living in outward conformity to "the king's religion;" but remembering her talk with François before he went away, she could believe that through all the cloud and darkness of Catholic ritual God would preserve the true faith in their hearts, and by and by, when they were free to leave the convent, He would enable them to escape to England, where they would once more be reunited in the pure and simple worship of the Reformed Church.

This was the constant prayer of her heart, and the hope that sustained her through all her difficulties and trials, for her life at Nîmes was altogether a new and strange experience to her, and very bitter at first.

At St. Etienne society had been divided into Huguenot and Catholic, but beyond this they knew nothing of social distinctions, and it probably was the same at other places where persecution had compelled people of one faith to cling together for mutual help and protection; but there was very little of this spirit remaining at Nîmes now, and Madame Marot was soon made to feel that her coming was a great annoyance to her brother-in-law's fashionable family. They were Huguenots, of course, but their religion had grown to be a secondary matter. To dress well, keep a good table, and maintain their position as citizens of Nîmes, was the first consideration; and to have a sister-in-law come among them who knew nothing of the nice distinctions of society, but thought that because she was of the same faith and in trouble she was to be treated with especial consideration, was preposterous. This was Jules Marot's way of putting it. In reality, poor Madame Marot made no demands upon her fashionable relatives, but she did expect a little kindness and sympathy, and not to be told that she must go and live at the other end of the town, where the houses were smaller and the rents cheaper, as soon as she arrived. A little kindly advice, a little gentle sympathy, would have saved her much anxiety and many heartaches; for, remembering the fate of her boys, the poor woman could scarcely be persuaded to trust Ninon or the other children out of her sight, and forbade them speaking to or answering a stranger if she was not near.

At Nîmes

So it was a very lonely life she led in a little back street of the city, which often made her long for the sweet, pure air of the hills, and the neighborly kindness common among the villagers of St. Etienne.

Even the visits of her husband, when he came to replenish his pack and stay for a few days' rest, afforded her little comfort. One time he told of his pack being upset, when it was discovered that he carried Huguenot books underneath his ribbons and laces, and in the confusion he lost his own book, which fell out of his pocket while he was gathering up the rest of his property.

"Never mind," said Madame Marot cheerfully; "God may direct that book to be the help and comfort of some poor starving soul. Let us pray that it may be so," she added. But her husband turned away in despair, no longer able to share her desire to "be careful for nothing, but in everything to make her requests known unto God."[1]

---

[1] PHILIPPIANS 4:6

He had lost this clue to a happy life, and knew not that it was the secret of his wife's cheerful content—ah! and of her usefulness too; for the sure trust she had, that God would preserve her boys' faith, and bring them back to her again, urged her nimble fingers to greater skill and quickness, that she might earn and save money to carry them all to England, when the time came. How this was to be accomplished was not her concern; she had committed her way unto God, and He would direct her path, making the crooked straight, and the rough places smooth. Her duty now was to pray, and wait, and work, guarding carefully the children God had left to her, lest they also should be entrapped into making a profession of "the king's religion."

This watching over and teaching her children was a great addition to her work. A great many Protestant schools had been closed at Nîmes, as well as in other places,

At Nîmes

and one of the first to be demolished was that in the poorest quarter of the town. Many parents were therefore compelled to teach their children themselves, if they did not wish them to grow up in ignorance, unless they were willing to send them to Catholic schools, an alternative which we may be sure Madame Marot never entertained for a moment.

So, while her nimble fingers twisted and wove the scarlet wool, one of the children would stand by her side, and spell out the words of a chapter in the New Testament, and then she would give her own simple explanation of it.

Frugal as their life at St. Etienne had been, the good mother contrived to make the *pot au feu* upon a still more economical plan now, that she might be able to add to the store of gold crowns she was saving for the expenses of their journey. This project was constantly kept before her mind by the news she heard, every now and again, of one and another of the neighbors going away.

There was no talk of it beforehand, but one night part of the family would go, and a few days afterwards the rest would follow. Marot told his wife that these migrations were now becoming so frequent among the Huguenots that the king was doing all he could to stop them. Sales of property had been forbidden; and in the event of anyone transgressing this law and afterwards leaving France, whatever had been disposed of was forfeited to the State.

But, in spite of this cruel and unjust law, the emigration of the Huguenots to England, Germany, and Geneva still went on steadily increasing, and Marot said he knew his brother was quietly transferring all the business to his branch house in Geneva. In the case of a merchant like Jules Marot this could be done without much loss or difficulty, more especially as the handicraftsmen were also leaving the country in

EMIGRATION: *moving to another country*

such numbers; but in the case of landowners, small farmers, vinedressers, and others who owned the plots of land they tilled, it meant almost absolute ruin to go away from France, as they could not sell their possessions now.

"It is a comfort we never bought a farm," Claude said one day, when he was talking this over with his wife. "Jules is leaving, I know, and you may be sent for any day to go and live at their house, and keep things going for a time, as though they were coming back again after a holiday; but once he has got his children safe over the border, they will never come back to be entrapped into a convent school, I know."

"And we will go, too, some day," said Madame Marot hopefully. "God will open a way for us when our boys are ready."

"I shall never leave France," her husband said gloomily.

"Nay, nay, Claude; but if our boys could go with us—" began his wife.

But he would not hear what she wanted to say. "You forget our boys are Catholics, and liable to imprisonment or even death as relapsed heretics, if they turned to the faith of their fathers now," he said hastily.

"But in England, Claude—nothing could hinder them from worshiping God according to their own conscience there," she said eagerly.

"It is not likely our boys will care anything about it when the priest and monks have done with them. No, no, Babette, you cannot hope for that. See, some of our own pastors have turned Catholics, to secure the reward offered to them; and as for our lawyers and doctors, why, they must take the king's creed or starve; and so, to expect two lads brought up among priests and monks to hold the Huguenot faith still, is—is to expect a miracle; and these are not the days of miracles," concluded Marot.

"Well, let me say this, Claude," said his

At Nîmes

wife: "I believe God will give us back our boys, and it may be we shall need to leave France while you are on one of your journeys. If it should be so, go to Jules' house in Geneva as quickly as you can, for I will send to him, or go there, if I should need to leave France."

"You—leave—France?" slowly uttered her husband, in amazement. He could scarcely believe it was his own Babette talking thus coolly of what was a dangerous enterprise even for experienced travelers.

The truth was, the removal to Nîmes had been of great service to Madame Marot, in teaching her many things she had never needed to learn in the little village among the hills; and the self-reliance, added to the implicit trust in God that her trials here had evoked, had greatly strengthened her character.

It was well that her husband had prepared her for a possible summons from her

IMPLICIT: *unquestioning*
EVOKED: *produced*

brother-in-law, for a few weeks afterwards Jules Marot sent for her to his office one morning, and then told her he was going to take his wife and daughters for a holiday to a distant part of France, and they wanted her to come and take care of the house while they were gone.

Madame Marot, remembering what her husband had said, knew well enough what this meant; but she readily agreed to do what was wished, as it would cover their flight for a time, and enable them to get to a place of refuge.

"The house is my own, you know, Babette, and so you can bring your things here, and stay as long as you like, and save paying other rent," said the merchant significantly, when she was leaving.

"Thank you. When shall I come?" she asked.

"Tonight. I will send a cart for your goods at dusk." He did not ask her to go beyond

At Nîmes

the office; indeed, he seemed so busy and flurried as scarcely to have time to speak to her; and she went out without bidding him good-bye, thinking she should see him again in the evening. But when she and the children, and their few possessions, reached the house soon after dark, an old man met her and told her Jules Marot had gone.

"Gone? and Madame too?" she uttered in surprise.

"Come in, come in!" said the old man. "This must not be talked of yet. I am going to open the office tomorrow, and carry on a little business if I can; but Monsieur Marot will never come back to France again. Madame went a fortnight ago, and her daughters last week; yesterday we heard they had safely reached the home that has been prepared for them in Geneva. So here we can stay as long as we like, or until it is found out my master has gone, and then all he has left behind him will be seized; but it will

A FORTNIGHT: *two weeks*

not be much they will get," chuckled the old man.

Indeed, it was not much that was left behind—at least, in the way of furniture—for everything but the very heaviest and most cumbersome had been taken away; and she heard that, for months past, Jules Marot had been slowly transferring his business and possessions, and helping his employees to emigrate to Geneva.

It was well Madame Marot had brought her few possessions with her, for except the curtains at the windows the rooms were almost bare, and she began to wish she had not agreed to come, for this large, empty house had a very cheerless appearance, after the cozy home she had made for herself at the other end of the town.

But after the children's beds were made, and a fire in the stove lighted, things began to look more comfortable, and she decided to stay here as long as she could; for it might

CUMBERSOME: *difficult to carry*

be that she should hear of her boys through the old clerk in the office, and this thought was sufficient to reconcile her to any discomfort.

Chapter VIII

The Escape

SLOWLY but surely the years slipped away at the convent, and, strange to say, the hope that had grown to be the very life of Madame Marot had begun to cheer the dreary routine of the days in the convent too. Father Eustace had first hinted it to Jacques, as an incentive to his persevering in learning all the art and mystery of silk-weaving. Jacques had shown great aptitude at first; but once the preliminary details had been mastered, his industry flagged.

"What is the good of trying?" he said, when Father Eustace spoke to him about this.

Then the young monk whispered a word

INCENTIVE: *motivation*
APTITUDE: *ability*
PRELIMINARY: *beginning*

The Escape

in his ear. "Have you no wish to go to England?" he said.

"To England!" said Jacques. "Will they banish us to England?"

"The Huguenots are flying there, and carrying their trade and industry with them, for it is whispered the king will revoke the Edict of Nantes, which he has always hated, as soon as it is safe to do so."

"But—but what has that to do with us in the convent?" asked Jacques.

"You will not always remain here. So soon as you are soundly Catholic, and have forgotten all you learned before you came, the doors will be opened for you. Huguenot children cannot be kept here always."

"I wish they would do it at once, then," grumbled Jacques. "I shall never be soundly Catholic, and so it is useless to wait for that."

"But you will be kept the longer, my son; and therefore I say, learn this silk-weaving,

INDUSTRY: *diligence*
FLAGGED: *faltered*
FLYING: *fleeing*

and by and by we will escape, and fly to England."

"Escape? Who do you mean?" gasped Jacques.

"You and I and François," said the young monk. "Your book has taught me much, my son, and I would fain learn more concerning this faith in the Lord Jesus Christ alone. This is the difference, as I conceive, between Huguenots and Catholics: you have faith in the Lord Jesus Christ only; you say that through His death you have redemption, without the help of saints or angels, or even the Blessed Virgin."

Jacques Marot looked amazed as the young monk made this clear declaration of faith.

"How did you learn to be a Huguenot here?" he said.

Father Eustace looked at him and smiled.

"I wonder what I should have done if you had not come here," he said, "and I had not had your book to help me."

WOULD FAIN: *desire to*

The Escape

"But—but I don't understand," said Jacques.

"No, I suppose not. It was not the book only, but the Spirit of God moving in my heart first. I came here to seek rest for my soul, pardon for my sins; but I found it not in services to the Virgin, or masses, or anything I could do, but your book said, 'God so loved the world, that He gave His only begotten Son, that whosoever believeth in Him should not perish, but have everlasting life.'[1] It was hard to believe at first, for my heart was full of sin, and I had so long been laboring to cast it out without avail, that it was not easy to believe the blessed words at first. But light came into my dark soul at last, and I saw that the Lord Christ had done for me what I could never do for myself. He had died to redeem me, and offered me a free salvation from sin, if I would accept Him to be my Savior. Ah, Jacques, I have wondered sometimes whether you had ever

[1] JOHN 3:16

tasted this blessedness, Huguenot though you were."

The lad hung his head, for in truth he knew little of this inner spiritual life as yet, although he had contrived to maintain his hold of the Huguenot teaching he had received in his early days, and by remembering the message brought to him from his mother he had made even the services in the chapel stepping-stones to God; for through these veils and clouds his heart had often ascended in prayer, and he had begun to long for the simpler, purer Huguenot services that he had scarcely valued in his younger days. To hear, therefore, that there was a possibility of escape from this dreary, stifled life in the convent, was enough to stimulate Jacques to renewed exertions at the loom, as well as to urge François to greater industry.

"How shall we escape? When shall we get away?" he asked eagerly.

But to this the young monk could only

shake his head. "I know not yet, my son, but I do and will believe that God will open a way for us in His own good time. We are not ready yet, even if the way was opened. You and I must master the weaving, my son, before we think of flying to England, and François too must perfect himself as much as possible."

If it could only have been known, the young monk was even more eager than Jacques to get away from the convent now for he longed to know more of this free spiritual life, and what the Huguenots could teach him concerning it.

At first, he thought the knowledge he had gained from reading the Gospel would be sufficient to sustain him. The rest he had longed for, the aspiration of his soul was satisfied, and he could believe that the Lord Jesus Christ was all-sufficient to redeem and to sanctify him, and in the joy of this new truth he could rest content for a little while.

ASPIRATION: *desire*
SANCTIFY HIM: *make him acceptable to God*

But by degrees the longing to make this known to others, and the impossibility of doing this while he was virtually a prisoner in the convent, added to the dissimulation he was constantly compelled to practice, to screen himself and the Marots from suspicion, made his life almost intolerable. He was compelled to join in rites and ceremonies in which he not only had no faith now, but which he believed were actually dishonoring to his Lord and Savior, and yet he dared not absent himself, for fear of cutting off all hope of freedom for himself and the lads.

The burden sometimes would have been greater than he could bear, had he not recalled the message sent by Madame Marot to her boy—that through these clouds and veils that concealed the face of God, he might yet look up to the very heart of the Father, who had loved him and sent His Son to die for him.

DISSIMULATION: *deception*

The Escape

How or when they were likely to effect an escape from the convent, that was almost as closely guarded as a prison, Father Eustace did not know; but he, like Madame Marot, worked and prayed constantly with this hope to bear him up through the present difficulties.

He knew well enough that there was little hope for Protestantism in France now, for every few months brought some fresh encroachment on the liberties of the Huguenots, and but for the great minister, Colbert, more active persecution would have been begun; and so to fly to some land of freedom was the only effectual way of escape. The door for this was opened at length in a most unexpected manner.

An epidemic broke out in the convent, and monks and pupils alike fell victims to its ravages, until at last an order came that all those not yet attacked should at once be sent to different places; and Father Eustace was

ENCROACHMENT ON: *taking of*
EFFECTUAL: *effective*
RAVAGES: *destruction*

deputed to take charge of Jacques, François, and half a dozen other lads, and convey them to a country house at some distance. It was summertime, and, with well-filled wallets, the walk of a dozen miles was like a picnic of pleasure to the emancipated boys. They ran and skipped along, chatting, laughing, and playing jokes upon each other; and no one seeing them or their guardian would have thought that any serious matter could just then have been entertained by any of them.

But Father Eustace and Jacques had exchanged glances and a few whispered words, and both knew that the momentous time had come for which they had been praying, and working, and waiting. The country house had been placed at the disposal of the prior by a nobleman who was going to Paris to escape from the prevailing sickness, and one or two old servants had been left in charge to render what assistance was needed by the newcomers. Now the point that

DEPUTED: *assigned*
WALLETS: *knapsacks*
EMANCIPATED: *freed from confinement*

The Escape 133

Father Eustace had to consider was, whether he should take all the lads on to this place of refuge, or leave them to find their way by themselves for the last mile or two, and make good his escape with Jacques and his brother at once.

Happily the point was settled for him when their journey was about half accomplished, for François caught his foot in a stone as they were fording a little stream, and fell flat into it. At first everybody laughed, for the brook was only deep enough to give him a thorough wetting; but as he was helped up and attempted to stand, he almost screamed with pain, as his foot gave way under him, and he again slipped into the water. It was evidently no laughing matter now, for Father Eustace had to lift him up, and, with the help of Jacques, carry him across the brook and up the opposite bank. They looked at each other in consternation as they set him down on the grass, and gazed round in search of a place where they could get his clothes dried.

It seemed as though their hopes were to be frustrated just when they seemed nearest fulfillment; for how were they to effect their escape with such a helpless burden upon their hands as François now was? The lad lay groaning and shivering on the grass, while his elder brother and the monk looked at each other in helpless bewilderment. At length one of the other boys suggested that they should run across the fields in search of a cottage or inn where they might carry him. "And then, Father Eustace, you could go on with us and bring a carriage back and fetch Jacques and François," said their young adviser.

No better plan seemed to suggest itself, and so it was decided to adopt this, and the boys ran on ahead, looking all round in search of some habitation, while Father Eustace and Jacques slowly followed along the footpath, carrying their dripping burden between them.

François caught his foot in a stone!

The Escape

"What shall we do now?" said Jacques; for the three were left to themselves, and could freely express their anxiety.

"We can only trust in God, and see what He will do for us," said Father Eustace, with a sigh.

Presently the other boys came running back, with the news that there was a little inn, or *auberge*, a short distance along the road, and from the top of the bank they could see a town in the distance.

"We will go to the *auberge*," said Father Eustace decidedly; and they hastened on with all the speed possible, for poor François seemed in great pain, and Father Eustace began to fear he had dislocated his ankle. Fortunately he understood something of surgery, and as soon as they reached the *auberge* he proceeded to examine the injured foot. He soon found that, although very much swollen, it was only a sprain, that a few days' rest would set right; but he kept

SURGERY: *medicine*

this opinion to himself for the present. He found that the boys looked upon the accident as being much more serious than it really was, and he resolved not to remove this impression.

He settled with the landlord that Jacques should be left in charge of his brother to do all that was necessary for him, and having seen him comfortably put to bed he prepared to resume his journey with the rest.

"I shall come back as soon as possible, and help you with the nursing, Jacques," he said, loud enough for all to hear. Then he stepped back, and whispered to the brothers, "I think I see a way of escape now."

"We are close to Nîmes—close to my uncle's house," said Jacques; "I know this road quite well. Oh! come back quickly, Father Eustace, so that we may go there and get what we need for our journey."

He had been longing to say this ever since they reached the *auberge*, and he had looked out of the little lattice window along the road; but such caution was needful, if they were to make good their escape, that he had not dared to whisper the joyful secret until they were left to themselves.

It was indeed glorious news to Father Eustace, but he could only utter a fervent, "Thank God for His mercy to us!" and then hasten away with the other boys, for they still had a long walk before them, and this accident had hindered them too long already.

It was late at night before they reached their destination, but Father Eustace was up early the next morning, for he was anxious to return to the Marots with as little delay as possible.

To the old major domo of the household he left the charge of the boys, saying it was uncertain when he should return, as the injured lad must be his first care now.

"Yes, yes," said the old man, to whom the accident had been explained the night

LATTICE WINDOW: *window covered with thin, crossed strips of wood*
MAJOR DOMO: *butler or chief steward*

before; "make your mind easy about the boys here, they will be safe enough; do you take care of the sick lad yonder. I wish I had a carriage, that we could send and fetch him for you."

But Father Eustace shook his head.

"Better as it is," he said; for he had felt relieved to hear that the family needed every available carriage to transport them to Paris the night before.

The six miles' walk was soon accomplished, and Father Eustace was glad to hear, when he reached the *auberge*, that his charge was much better.

"I think I could walk to Nîmes, Father Eustace," said François.

"Not yet, not yet, my son; there is plenty of time," said the monk, whose heart beat high with hope this morning.

He examined the ankle, and found it very much better; and after bandaging it, he sat down to discuss with Jacques the best way to get to Nîmes.

The Escape

At last it was decided that Jacques should go that evening, but not venture to approach his uncle's house until dusk, for fear of being recognized; and then the lad grew eager for the hours to pass, for he was anxious to know whether his uncle would be willing to let them have the money necessary to make their escape.

The walk to Nîmes was quickly got over; and as the shades of evening fell, Jacques entered the town, and, choosing the least frequented streets, made his way to his uncle's house.

But his surprise may be imagined when, instead of a servant coming to the door, his mother herself stood before him. "Mother! Mother!" he gasped; but as he spoke he slipped inside and shut the door, for fear anyone should see and recognize him.

In a moment he was clasped in his mother's arms, and she was murmuring heartfelt thanksgivings to God; but her next words were, "Where is François?"

SHADES: *shadows*

"Close by, Mother. We want to get away from the convent, away from France to England, where Father Eustace says we can worship God as we please. Can my uncle help us?" he asked anxiously, as he looked round the almost bare room, which he remembered to have been so handsomely furnished the last time he was there.

"Your uncle has left France; but I can help you, my boy," said Madame Marot joyfully. "I knew God would answer my prayers, and suffer you to escape 'from the snare of the fowler;'[1] and for this I have been working and saving, even while I prayed." And as she spoke she took a large key from her girdle, and unlocked a carved oak chest that was fixed in a recess of the wall, and took from it a leather purse containing a good supply of money.

"See! there is enough to pay for our journey to England. Your father has been making inquiries while on his travels, and—"

---

[1] PSALM 91:3
SUFFER: *allow*
GIRDLE: *belt*

The Escape 143

"But there is Father Eustace—I cannot go without him, Mother," interrupted Jacques.

"Father Eustace—a monk—to go with us!" exclaimed Madame Marot in dismay.

"Yes, Mother, he is a monk, but he has learned to be a Huguenot as much as we are, through Father's old Gospel of John, and now he is anxious to serve God as we do." And then some further explanations had to be given about Father Eustace, and how he had befriended them all the time they were in the convent.

But it was hard at first to make Madame Marot believe that all this could have been done in sincerity by a monk. She had heard so many tales of treachery that she had grown suspicious of late, and the fact that this monk still had her youngest boy in his power made her more unwilling to believe in his truth and sincerity.

"I am afraid it is all a trick to betray us," she said, with a groan.

"A trick! Father Eustace play us a trick! Mother, I would rather trust Father Eustace than my uncle," said Jacques solemnly. "I wish you could see him, Mother. He is so different from all the other monks, so gentle and serious. I believe the rest suspected him of helping to keep us in mind of what you had taught us. I know they did not like him, and he can never learn all he wants to know while he is a monk, and that is why he wants to go to London and be a silk-weaver. We have all learnt silk-weaving," added Jacques.

It was hard for the mother to trust in the goodwill of a monk, but at last Jacques suggested that she should go with him to the *auberge,* and see François and Father Eustace for herself. Ninon could be trusted to take care of the children.

But while they were discussing this there came another knock at the door, and on opening it, Marot was seen standing in the entry with his pack.

The Escape

"Claude, Claude! Jacques is here, and François is not far off, only he has hurt his foot, and a monk is staying with him at an inn close by."

Marot looked as though he did not understand, until Jacques ran forward and embraced him. "We want to go to England, Father; we don't mean to go back to the convent again; we are as much Huguenot now as ever we were."

The father put his hand across his brow, as if to lift a weight from his head, as he leaned against the wall beside his pack. "My God has not forsaken me, then!" he slowly uttered; and then, strong man as he was, he burst into tears and sobbed on the head of his son.

Strange to say, it was less difficult to make his father believe in the sincerity of the monk's goodwill towards them. Marot readily agreed to go to the inn the next morning, and consult with Father Eustace as to the best mode of escape and the disguise to be adopted.

The knowledge of the world gained in his travels was of great use to Marot now; and when he understood how they had left the convent, and that a search would inevitably be set on foot in a few days, he saw that their only chance of escape was to get away as speedily as possible.

So it was arranged that Father Eustace should leave the *auberge* the next day with the boys, and when they reached a village near the seacoast, he should don the attire of a peddler, and take charge of Marot's pack, until they reached their destination.

It was agreed that the whole family should meet at this village—not to travel together, that would tend to excite suspicion, but to assume different disguises, and wend their way by various routes to two different ports, where they might find a vessel bound for England.

WEND: *make*

The Escape

The Huguenot colony in London was ready to receive and help any who could escape from priest-dominated France, and this was to be the destination of the three groups into which the family was broken up.

After weeks of anxious separation, they met once more in that northeast corner of London that had already become like the quarter of a French town; for here was already settled a large community of silk-weavers, who had set up their looms, and were plying a flourishing trade in ribbons, silks, and velvets.

Here they met, and for the first time in many years knelt at the throne of God without fear of being torn asunder or accused of breaking some law by the exercise of their religious service.

Here they could walk in the Spital Fields, and sing the hymns of their ancestor, Marot, as freely as the birds in the hedgerow; and although their English neighbors seemed

SPITAL FIELDS: *an area of London, named for the hospital that once stood on the site, where many Huguenot families settled* cold and stiff in their manners, still they were kind and hospitable to these French emigrants, and were quite willing to extend to them the liberty they so dearly loved themselves.

Father Eustace never resumed the habit of a monk, but resigning his peddler's dress to Marot, adopted the attire and occupation of a silk-weaver, which he and Jacques plied with such industry that another comfortable French home was speedily added to the fast-growing colony clustered round the old priory of St. Helens. As the years went on, and the King of France in his great folly revoked the famous Edict of Nantes, which was the charter of liberty for the Protestant Church, in 1685, the French colony in London and in many other English towns was greatly increased.

By this act of oppressive cruelty, Louis XIV drove nearly all the most skillful and industrious artisans out of the kingdom, or

HABIT: *robe*
PLIED: *worked*
PRIORY: *monastery*

consigned them to imprisonment and death, unless they would conform to the king's religion. Alas! too many were ready to do this, for worldly prosperity had been a time of spiritual decay to not a few who were yet proud to call themselves Huguenots.

But God sent this judgment in mercy, and many who had slumbered and slept in this time of ease were aroused by this calamity to lay hold of God and His truth as they had never done before. Fierce and hot blew the whirlwind of persecution, but many were found ready to forsake all that makes life dear—to yield even life itself—rather than turn from the truth of God to the lies of Romanism, and so won that crown of martyrdom, and their Savior-King's commendation, "Well done, good and faithful servant... enter thou into the joy of thy Lord."[1]

The End

[1] MATTHEW 25:23

CONSIGNED: *condemned*

ABOUT THE AUTHOR

Emma Leslie (1837-1909), whose actual name was Emma Dixon, lived in Lewisham, Kent, in the south of England. She was a prolific Victorian children's author who wrote over 100 books. Emma Leslie's first book, *The Two Orphans*, was published in 1863 and her books remained in print for years after her death. She is buried at the St. Mary's Parish Church, in Pwllcrochan, Pembroke, South Wales.

Emma Leslie brought a strong Christian emphasis into her writing and many of her books were published by the Religious Tract Society. Her extensive historical fiction works covered many important periods in church history. Her writing also included a short booklet on the life of Queen Victoria published in the 50th year of the Queen's reign.

More Church History for Younger Readers

The Magic Runes
A Tale of the Times of Charlemagne
by Emma Leslie
Illustrated by J. W. D. & P. N. S.

One day, in 782 A.D., young Adalinda is startled to come upon a Saxon family in the forest where she lives with her father. The family is in desperate need but the husband, Godrith, is suspicious of Adalinda's offers of help, especially when he learns that she is a Christian. He well remembers how Charlemagne's "Christian" soldiers burned his village and killed or captured so many of his people because they refused to convert to Christianity. Will Adalinda and her father be able to show Godrith a different picture of Christianity?

www.SalemRidgePress.com

More Church History for Younger Readers

SOLDIER FRITZ
A Story of the Reformation
by Emma Leslie
Illustrated by C. A. Ferrier

Young Fritz wants to follow in the footsteps of Martin Luther and be a soldier for the Lord, so he chooses a Bible from the peddler's pack as his birthday gift. When his father, the Count, goes off to war, however, Fritz and his mother and little sister are forced to flee into the forest to escape being thrown in prison for their new faith. Disguising themselves as commoners, they must trust the Lord as they wait and hope for the Count to rescue them. But how will he ever be able to find them?

www.SalemRidgePress.com

Emma Leslie Church History Series

GLAUCIA THE GREEK SLAVE
A Tale of Athens in the First Century

After the death of her father, Glaucia is sold to a wealthy Roman family to pay his debts. She tries hard to adjust to her new life but longs to find a God who can love even a slave. Meanwhile, her brother, Laon, struggles to find her and to earn enough money to buy her freedom. But what is the mystery that surrounds their mother's disappearance years earlier and will they ever be able to read the message in the parchments she left for them?

THE CAPTIVES
Or, Escape from the Druid Council

The Druid priests are as cold and cruel as the forest spirits they claim to represent, and Guntra, the chief of her tribe of Britons, must make a desperate deal with them to protect those she loves. Unaware of Guntra's struggles, Jugurtha, her son, longs to drive the hated Roman conquerors from the land. When he encounters the Christian centurion, Marcinius, Jugurtha mocks the idea of a God of love and kindness, but there comes a day when he is in need of love and kindness for himself and his beloved little sister. Will he allow Marcinius to help him? And will the gospel of Jesus Christ ever penetrate the brutal religion of the proud Britons?

www.SalemRidgePress.com

Emma Leslie Church History Series

OUT OF THE MOUTH OF THE LION
Or, The Church in the Catacombs

When Flaminius, a high Roman official, takes his wife, Flavia, to the Colosseum to see Christians thrown to the lions, he has no idea the effect it will have. Flavia cannot forget the faith of the martyrs, and finally, to protect her from complete disgrace or even danger, Flaminius requests a transfer to a more remote government post. As he and his family travel to the seven cities of Asia Minor mentioned in Revelation, he sees the various responses of the churches to persecution. His attitude toward the despised Christians begins to change, but does he dare forsake the gods of Rome and embrace the Lord Jesus Christ?

SOWING BESIDE ALL WATERS
A Tale of the World in the Church

There is newfound freedom from persecution for Christians under the emperor, Constantine, but newfound troubles as well. Errors and pagan ways are creeping into the Church, while many of the most devoted Christians are withdrawing from the world into the desert as hermits and nuns. Quadratus, one of the emperor's special guards, is concerned over these developments, even in his own family. Then a riot sweeps through the city and Quadratus' home is ransacked. When he regains consciousness, he finds that his sister, Placidia, is gone. Where is she? And can the Church handle the new freedom, and remain faithful?

www.SalemRidgePress.com

Emma Leslie Church History Series

FROM BONDAGE TO FREEDOM
A Tale of the Times of Mohammed

At a Syrian market two Christian women are sold as slaves. One of the slaves ends up in Rome where Bishop Gregory is teaching his new doctrine of "purgatory" and the need for Christians to finish paying for their own sins. The other slave travels with her new master, Mohammed, back to Arabia, where Mohammed eventually declares himself to be the prophet of God. In Rome and Arabia, the two women and countless others fall into the bondage of man-made religions—will they learn at last to find true freedom in the Lord Jesus Christ alone?

THE MARTYR'S VICTORY
A Story of Danish England

Knowing full well they may die in the attempt, a small band of monks sets out to convert the savage Danes who have laid waste to the surrounding countryside year after year. The monks' faith is sorely tested as they face opposition from the angry Priest of Odin as well as doubts, sickness and starvation, but their leader, Osric, is unwavering in his attempts to share the "White Christ" with those who reject Him. Then the monks discover a young Christian woman who has escaped being sacrificed to the Danish gods—can she help reach those who had enslaved her and tried to kill her?

GYTHA'S MESSAGE
A Tale of Saxon England

Having discovered God's love for her, Gytha, a young slave, longs to escape the violence and cruelty of the world and devote herself to learning more about this God of love. Instead she lives in a Saxon household that despises the name of Christ. Her simple faith and devoted service bring hope and purpose to those around her, especially during the dark days when England is defeated by William the Conqueror. Through all of her trials, can Gytha learn to trust that God often has greater work for us to do *in* the world than *out* of it?

www.SalemRidgePress.com

Emma Leslie Church History Series

LEOFWINE THE MONK
Or, The Curse of the Ericsons
A Story of a Saxon Family

Leofwine, unlike his wild, younger brother, finds no pleasure in terrorizing the countrside, and longs to enter a monastery. Shortly after he does, however, he hears strange rumors of a monk who preaches "heresy". Unable to stop thinking about these new ideas, Leofwine at last determines to leave the monastery and England. Leofwine's search for inner peace takes him to France and Rome and finally to Jerusalem, but in his travels, he uncovers a plot against his beloved country. Will he be able to help save England? And will he ever find true rest for his troubled soul?

ELFREDA THE SAXON
Or, The Orphan of Jerusalem
A Sequel to Leofwine

When Jerusalem is captured by the Muslims, Elfreda, a young orphan, is sent back to England to her mother's sister. Her aunt is not at all pleased to see her, and her uncle fears she may have brought the family curse back to England. Elfreda's cousin, Guy, who is joining King Richard's Crusade, promises Elfreda that he will win such honor as a crusader that the curse will be removed. Over the years that follow, however, severe trials befall the family and Guy and Elfreda despair of the curse ever being lifted. Is it possible that there is One with power stronger than any curse?

DEARER THAN LIFE
A Story of the Times of Wycliffe

When a neighboring monastery lays claim to one of his fields, Sir Hugh Middleton refuses to yield his property, and further offends the monastery by sending his younger son, Stephen, to study under Dr. John Wycliffe. At the same time, Sir Hugh sends his elder son, Harry, to serve as an attendant to the powerful Duke of Lancaster. As Wycliffe seeks to share the Word of God with the common people, Stephen and Harry and their sisters help spread the truth, but what will it cost them in the dangerous day in which they live?

www.SalemRidgePress.com

Emma Leslie Church History Series

BEFORE THE DAWN
A Tale of Wycliffe and Huss

To please her crippled grandson, Conrad, Dame Ursula allows a kindly blacksmith and his friend, Ned Trueman, to visit the boy. Soon, however, she becomes suspicious that the men belong to the despised group who are followers of Dr. John Wycliffe, and she passionately warns Conrad of the dangers of evil "heresy". He decides to become a famous teacher in the Church so he can combat heresy, but he wonders why all the remedies of the Church fail to cure him. And why do his mother and grandmother refuse to speak of the father he has never known?

FAITHFUL, BUT NOT FAMOUS
A Tale of the French Reformation

Young Claude Leclerc travels to Paris to begin his training for the priesthood, but he is not sure *what* he believes about God. One day he learns the words to an old hymn and is drawn to the lines about "David's Royal Fountain" that will "purge every sin away." Claude yearns to find this fountain, and at last dares to ask the famous Dr. Lefèvre where he can find it. His question leads Dr. Lefèvre to set aside his study of the saints and study the Scriptures in earnest. As Dr. Lefèvre grasps the wonderful truth of salvation by grace, he wants to share it with Claude, but Claude has mysteriously disappeared. Where is he? And is France truly ready to receive the good news of the gospel of Jesus Christ?

www.SalemRidgePress.com

Additional Titles Available From
Salem Ridge Press

DOWN THE SNOW STAIRS
Or, From Goodnight to Goodmorning
by Alice Corkran
Illustrated by Gordon Browne R. I.

On Christmas Eve, eight-year-old Kitty cannot sleep, knowing that her beloved little brother is critically ill due to her own disobedience. Traveling in a dream to Naughty Children Land, she meets many strange people, including Daddy Coax and Lady Love. Kitty longs to return to the Path of Obedience but can she resist the many temptations she faces? Will she find her way home in time for Christmas? An imaginative and delightful read-aloud for the whole family!

YOUNG ROBIN HOOD
by George Manville Fenn
Illustrated by Victor Venner

In the days of Robin Hood, a young boy named Robin is journeying through Sherwood Forest when suddenly the company is surrounded by men in green. Deserted in the commotion by an unfaithful servant, Robin finds himself alone in the forest. After a miserable night, Robin is found by Little John. Robin is treated kindly by Robin Hood, Maid Marian and the Merry Men, but how long must he wait for his father, the Sheriff of Nottingham, to come to take him home?

www.SalemRidgePress.com

Fiction for Younger Readers

MARY JANE – HER BOOK
by Clara Ingram Judson
Illustrated by Francis White

This story, the first book in the Mary Jane series, recounts the happy, wholesome adventures of five-year-old Mary Jane and her family as she helps her mother around the house, goes on a picnic with the big girls, plants a garden with her father, learns to sew and more!

MARY JANE – HER VISIT
by Clara Ingram Judson
Illustrated by Francis White

In this story, the second book in the Mary Jane series, five-year-old Mary Jane has more happy, wholesome adventures, this time at her great-grandparents' farm in the country where she hunts for eggs, picks berries, finds baby rabbits, goes to the circus and more!

www.SalemRidgePress.com

Historical Fiction for Younger Readers

AMERICAN TWINS OF THE REVOLUTION
by Lucy Fitch Perkins

General Washington has no money to pay his discouraged troops and twins Sally and Roger are asked by their father, General Priestly, to help hide a shipment of gold which will be used to pay the American soldiers. Unfortunately, British spies have also learned about the gold and will stop at nothing to prevent it from reaching General Washington. Based on a true story, this is a thrilling episode from our nation's history!

MARIE'S HOME
Or, A Glimpse of the Past
by Caroline Austin
Illustrated by Gordon Browne R. I.

Eleven-year-old Marie Hamilton and her family travel to France at the invitation of Louis XVI, just before the start of the French Revolution. There they encounter the tremendous disparity between the proud French Nobility and the oppressed and starving French people. When an enraged mob storms the palace of Versailles, Marie and her family are rescued from grave danger by a strange twist of events, but Marie's story of courage, self-sacrifice and true nobility is not yet over! Honor, duty, compassion and forgiveness are all portrayed in this uplifting story.

www.SalemRidgePress.com

Historical Fiction by William W. Canfield

THE WHITE SENECA
Illustrated by G. A. Harker

Captured by the Senecas, fifteen-year-old Henry Cochrane grows to love the Indian ways and becomes Dundiswa—the White Seneca. When Henry is captured by an enemy tribe, however, he must make a desperate attempt to escape from them and rescue fellow captive, Constance Leonard. He will need all the skills he has learned from the Indians, as well as great courage and determination, if he is to succeed. But what will happen to the young woman if they do reach safety? And will he ever be able to return to his own people?

AT SENECA CASTLE
Illustrated by G. A. Harker

In this sequel to *The White Seneca*, Henry Cochrane, now eighteen, faces many perils as he serves as a scout for the Continental Army. General Washington is determined to do whatever it takes to stop the constant Indian attacks on the settlers and yet Henry is torn between his love for the Senecas and his loyalty to his own people. As the Army advances across New York State, Henry receives permission to travel ahead and warn his Indian friends of the coming destruction. But will he reach them in time? And what has happened to the beautiful Constance Leonard whom he had been forced to leave in captivity a year earlier?

THE SIGN ABOVE THE DOOR

Young Prince Martiesen is ruler of the land of Goshen in Egypt, where the Hebrews live. Eight plagues have already come upon Egypt and now Martiesen has been forced by Pharaoh to further increase the burden of the Hebrews. Martiesen, however, is in love with the beautiful Hebrew maiden, Elisheba, whom he is forbidden by Egyptian law to marry. As the nation despairs, the other nobles turn to Martiesen for leadership, but before he can decide what to do, Elisheba is kidnapped by the evil Peshala and terrifying darkness falls over the land. An exciting tale woven around the events of the Exodus from the Egyptian perspective!

www.SalemRidgePress.com

Adventure by George Manville Fenn

YUSSUF THE GUIDE
Being the Strange Story of the Travels in Asia Minor of Burne the Lawyer, Preston the Professor, and Lawrence the Sick
Illustrated by John Schönberg

Young Lawrence, an invalid, convinces his guardians, Preston the Professor and Burne the Lawyer, to take him along on an archaeological expedition to Turkey. Before they set out, they engage Yussuf as their guide. Through the months that follow, the friends travel deeper and deeper into the remote regions of central Turkey on their trusty horses in search of ancient ruins. Yussuf proves his worth time and time again as they face dangers from a murderous ship captain, poisonous snakes, sheer precipices, bands of robbers and more. Memorable characters, humor and adventure abound in this exciting story!

www.SalemRidgePress.com

www.ingramcontent.com/pod-product-compliance
Lightning Source LLC
Chambersburg PA
CBHW032357040426
42451CB00006B/44